D1244674

My Son Connor

FORWARD PUBLISHING
MINNEAPOLIS, MINNESOTA

My Son Connor

Life Lessons Learned From My Special-Needs Son Diagnosed With Williams Syndrome That Will Benefit Your Life And Your Work

By Michael A. Boylan

Forward Publishing
Minneapolis, Minnesota

Published by Forward Publishing, a wholly owned subsidary of Forward Communications LLC. Carlson Center, 601 Carlson Parkway, Suite 1050, Minnetonka, Minnesota, 55305, U.S.A.

Office: 952-449-5115 Fax: 952–856-4898
Web Site: www.Forward–Communications.com

First published in 2009 by Forward Publishing.
Official publication date: September, 2009

10 9 8 7 6 5 4 3 2 1

Library of Congress Cataloging-in-Publication Data

Cover design and layout by Megan French
Print Production by P.H. Lanpher and Associates
Photographs by Robert Boylan

ISBN Number 978–0–9822163–0–9
First Edition, Hardcover, September, 2009

Printed in the United States of America

This book is dedicated to my son Connor and my daughter Courtney, the apples of my eyes and heart. From them I have learned much about love, suffering, service, and gentleness—attributes so important and necessary for the raising of our children and desperately needed in the workplace, as all too often, it seems as if it's *all* about the dollar.

I also dedicate this work to the *millions* of parents and families caring for their special-needs children. You are not alone, though you may feel that way, as I do when things get really tough and there doesn't seem to be any end in sight. It is so easy to feel all by yourself when you are the parent of a special-needs child. It's overwhelmingly difficult sometimes, emotionally and psychologically—and lonely.

This book is *not* about finding a cure or focusing awareness on any one particular special need, nor on potential causes or contributors to any one special need. There are several books that focus their energies in this vein raising the general consciousness, which is absolutely needed. By sharing my story and experience as the single father of a special-needs child—offering it up and putting it out there, my hope is it will provide encouragement and inspiration for the *millions* of caregivers of special-needs children throughout the world. That's right, *millions*.

My goal with this book and our work through *The Reach For Me Network*™ throughout the country and eventually, around the world, is to take better care of the caregivers so they are emotionally supported and empowered to provide better care for their special-needs children, and feel better about themselves in the process. The world community needs to become aware, look up to, and honor the courage, conviction, and selfless humility of caregivers for their unending emotional and physical care and love they give these children day after long day. I know of these emotions, struggles, stresses, and challenges firsthand as a caregiver.

Another goal of this work is to create a global dialog and deeper level of understanding and compassion within the numerous constituencies that are impacted and that *intersect* around the issue of caring for special-needs children: employer organizations, schools, the healthcare establishment, the life insurance, banking, and financial planning industries, pharmaceuticals, state and federal government programs, etc. They *all* need to understand at a deeper level the continuous hills and valleys of the caregiver's heart, mind, and spirit along the way. There's inner peace that can come from what these angels from above teach us, which as I am learning, can deepen the meaning, purpose, and joy within our own lives.

By offering this story about my situation and sharing the continuous journey we caregivers are on, and the principles I've come to learn from my son Connor, I hope you will feel a warm blanket of support from your extended family and friends as you go about your daily lives of providing care and attention to those who require much more of you because they have special needs.

I pray you experience a deep peace in your most challenging hours, with grace guiding your thoughts and actions as you learn to care on a deeper level, and cope with the situations that have entered your path.

I hope this book also inspires those who are dealing with a sudden or life-changing situation calling for massive strength and understanding just to hold things together as you cope with the host of emotions coming at you all at once. The loss of a child or spouse, job loss or change, sudden news of an illness, depression, anxiety, despair, or a general uncertainty about where your life is headed. I hope the principles I've learned from my mentally challenged son allow you to become more open to what the principles are really about, helping calm and center you as you look for a deeper meaning and purpose in those moments when you wonder if anyone cares or understands.

Open your heart as you let this true story and the principles that have come as a result of my life situation, experiences, ongoing learning and hardships help you in your everyday life to find a deeper meaning so you too can keep moving forward.

Be well, and move forward.

Michael A. Boylan

I have learned that writing is a gift often requiring the talents of others experienced in editing and preparing a work to be of value to others. It is with genuine gratitude that I therefore wish to thank the following people for assisting me with this work: Megan French for her cover design and layout expertise; Wendy Burt-Thomas for her talents around copy-editing and readability; Peter Lanpher for his expertise around print production; Robert Boylan, my father, for his many photos, which are contained throughout; my mother, brother, and three sisters for their encouragement through the dark and visionless years where I couldn't see anything positive ahead; Father Bob White and Father Arnold Weber for their great counsel, especially over the past four years; Dick Rice for walking with me every week—always ready to lend an ear; and several other close friends who encouraged me during the tough years––more of which are ahead. And to Connor's many wonderful therapists, teachers, paraprofessionals, and medical doctors for giving him their love, undivided attention, patience, and expertise in helping continue his progress.

I also want to thank in advance several media personalities who will interview Connor and me, helping foster a greater awareness of the millions of caregivers of special-needs children throughout the country and around the world who continue to give their lives for the well-being of their special-needs children.

Thank you for seeing why it's critical for our country, all businesses and industries, and the special-needs children, that caregivers get the emotional support and encouragement they need to *keep on going and moving forward*.

Remember, it's not a good thing if caregivers just give up and throw in the towel. In that scenario, we all lose! The caregivers, their families, the special-needs children, and all of us. In this scenario, we'd all pay the consequences through higher taxes to fund more government and statewide assistance-related programs. It's *common sense* therefore, that we understand the scope of what's going on around us when it comes to the far-reaching implications of this issue on millions of caregivers, the companies who employ them, governments, and societies.

Finally, I want to thank the one above for putting the song *Angel Child* into my head while jogging one cool fall morning in Minnesota. It came so fast I sat down at the piano to play what I was hearing in my head: a song inspiring me to write and arrange for an orchestra, then record in Los Angeles with a full orchestra and professional choir at the Warner Brothers Studio Sound Stage.

Thank you to all the musicians and singers involved, sound engineers, mixers, arrangers, and videographers who shot and edited the music video for *Angel Child*. They captured the emotions that need to be conveyed about what it can be like to be a caregiver of a special-needs child. See the video if you haven't already, and you may find a deeper level of understanding and compassion for those in your community who are caregivers to a special-needs child.

Nowadays, many of us are so busy, stressed out and wound up about all the important *stuff* we must deal with from one day to the next. Hence, we're all tight on time and want to know *right now* how this or that could help us, so we can decide where to invest our time, knowing the payoff will be there. Let me address that issue right now.

If you are a **parent** or family member caring for a special-needs child, this book was written for you and can help you. Credible research says **one** in **five** families in the U.S. is directly or indirectly caring for a special-needs child, which, if you do the math, means as many as **35 million** people in the U.S. alone are impacted and touched by a special-needs child. Globally, the number of caregivers impacted is even larger. A sizeable community of people experiencing various emotional, physical, financial, psychological, and spiritual challenges of worry, doubt, frustration, confusion, anger, anxiety, and despair on some level, quite frequently throughout their lives as their special-needs children grow up. This book will give you some comfort in knowing that you are definitely not alone, but in fact, part of an expanding global community of gifted people who've been *called* for an extra level of service to our children.

If you are going through a job loss or change, the principles in this book can also help you through your transition period. And, if you are coping with challenges with your children, friends, coworkers or boss, these principles provide a road map for arriving at resolutions, helping calm and center you, as you make sense of all the shuffling around you.

If you are searching for more balance and want a framework to help you resolve or handle the tough stuff that comes up throughout our lives, these timeless principles will endure. No trendy advise here, but rather principles full of common sense, dignity, and genuine respect.

Life is difficult at times because *people* can be very difficult, self-absorbed, overly fascinated with themselves, and unbending at times. I don't think this is negative thinking, but rather just a fact of life. It's a truism that we're all going to happen upon various speed bumps in the road of life. Sometimes they are downright miserable, but with time, things can come back. However, there are other speed bumps that cause *permanent* changes, where things might *never* return to the way they were. And for certain, these permanent bumps can seem unfair, overwhelming, and very unsettling—as if your compass for the right way forward doesn't exist anymore, forcing you to figure things out on your own. In these situations, who doesn't need some help or a little pick-me-up once in a while or reassurance that things are somehow going to work out, even though all you might feel at the moment is confusion, despair, anger, and total disbelief?

We all have moments when we wonder, *What the heck is going on? Why is this happening to me? Did I do something to deserve this? Why am I not catching any breaks? Are things going to get any better, or am I being punished?* These are all questions I wanted answers to ASAP when the sudden permanent news and events hit for me. But the answers didn't come that fast. Maybe that's the case with everyone. Or maybe in the waiting, we are being *shaped* and *prepared* for other purposes down the road that we have no idea are ahead. Nobody has a crystal ball, though it would sure be nice sometimes.

During our life, most of us will go through at least four sudden, un-expected, significant events or changes in our professional and personal life which, when they happen, tend to impact *everything* over time. When these things occur, we know there are three basic choices we can make:

1. Do nothing, tread water, mope, become angry, bitter, and effectively paralyzed to take any type of action—my case for years.
2. Go backwards, allowing the psyche to fixate, causing people and organizations to retrench and lose ground, or they can…
3. Go forward, dealing head-on with the circumstances, digesting, understanding, reframing, and finding new inspiration to move forward with a fresh perspective; allowing us to get past the tough stuff, becoming reenergized to take on the road ahead with a renewed spirit and peace, and to be of better service to others—in my case, to my special-needs child.

When traumatic things happen, the old expression *this too shall pass* just doesn't cut it for many folks—especially when the things happening are *permanent* changes to your personal and professional life—events that will impact your life forever.

In these times, trendy, temporary *fixes* will not suffice. We must rely on a set of guiding principles that can bring some level of peace and calm during the storm, helping pull you back up, out, and forward. This is the simple power of *The Connor Principles*™—principles that have application in personal and work-related situations; a common framework for dealing with challenging situations for the betterment of all involved.

What's unique about this book is that it's a true story about how my life changed instantly and forever with the birth of my special-needs son. There were no warnings, no preparations, and no guideposts to follow, leaving me feeling alone and full of anxiety. It's also about how our family came *unwound* with the struggles and hardships that took place as a result of learning to cope with new life pictures, pictures which had never entered my mind until everything hit all at once. It changed and eventually destroyed the relationship between my wife and me. It impacted the relationship with my daughter and our friends. It affected how we lived on a daily basis, coping as best we could while trying to learn how to care for Connor and handle *life* and work at the same time—a continuous challenge to this day.

I share the struggles and challenges of coping with a new life situation with a child that needs me to be present in the truest sense—mentally, emotionally, and physically—and how it *forced* a re-ordering of everything, work, travel, business relationships, friendships, attitudes, activities, my faith, beliefs, and feelings. And the constant fight within that is part of the process of trying to understand the questions I kept asking myself: *Why me? Why am I being singled out for this? I have no ability to do this! What the h… is going on? Who's in charge here? How am I supposed to get anything done in life?*

I offer these emotions, which I have struggled with, as honestly as I know how; challenges as a single father caring for my special-needs son. The process of total *surrender* to his needs, and the deep peace it has brought me in times of total confusion and despair.

Please understand that this is *not* a cry-in-your-beer, self-directed sob story. Instead, it's the truth about how this new life challenge pressed up against and challenged everything I had learned as a young man, forcing me to relax, chill out, open up, let go, and trust more than ever before that somehow things would be okay around this new life I am learning to adjust to as I write this book. I am learning a brand new way to deal with and be grateful for the challenges that are, at times, overwhelming, yet have also enlightened me, and many others. And believe it or not, they have made me a more complete person, and a better helper of others, because I have a much deeper level of understanding. It's as if an *angel* has been standing next to me the entire way, an angel child named Connor.

The Connor Principles™ are my lessons from a mentally challenged beautiful son who has taught me more about life—and what it's supposed to be about in a few short years than anything I've learned through schooling, athletic competition, business, friendships, my church, or just living. The principles are meant to serve as a living guide in those times when your world seems totally upside down and nothing fits, nothing is in order, and your attempts to bring things under control don't have any positive outcome—at least within the timeframe in which you wanted relief. They've been such a help to me since I was raised as an organized, can-do, motivated person focused on staying on track. And yet, I now ask myself, *Whose track?* because that style of living doesn't work for Connor. As a result, they've helped me learn how to change, serve, and remold my personality to accommodate what my son needs. That has been challenging, but ever rewarding.

My sincere desire is that you will use these principles in your time of need so you have less stress, a deeper peace, and a gentle grace guiding your thoughts, emotions, and actions as you deal with the challenges that have entered your path of life and work. Let this story and principles find their way to bettering your life.

—Michael A. Boylan

TABLE OF CONTENTS

All of us compare our *situations* to other people's situations and often determine how we feel about ours by comparison. We look to see if anyone's got it as tough as we do, or has as difficult a life. I do this, and I know parents of specials-needs children that do this as well. We *all* do. Some more than others because it can be very lonely when you are the primary caregiver and wonder if you'll hold up, just for that day. I don't know why we're like this. Maybe it's our way of coping with our feelings, frustrations, and fears, by comparing ourselves to who has it better or easier than us, to those who've got it much worse. So our pain, sorrows, confusion, and anger are justified in some respect.

When my situation hit, I truly felt as though I was the only person in the world dealing with such a difficult emotional and challenging road. I didn't know if I could handle it, or if I had the depth of patience, temperament, and the ability to earn a living while being a committed caregiver for my son. Could I be emotionally present for him in the manner he required for his progress and feelings of self-worth, since his spirit is *so* sensitive emotionally? These were huge things for me to learn, and I am still learning them.

Parents and families of special-needs children are a unique and special community of people who have been handed lifelong situations that are not only challenging, but also very hard emotionally, psychologically, and sometimes spiritually, day in and day out, because they cut to the *core* of what we are about really—our children; what we want for them and for ourselves. And it challenges many of the early life pictures and expectations of what *we* want out of life. Sometimes, it deals us life-changing news so hard to accept that it takes a lifetime to adjust. Perhaps it's similar to someone suffering from depression, anxiety, or another life illness or situation such as an addiction to chemicals, or work.

Based on my experience of giving, and giving, and giving care, love, total focused attention and a calm heart to my son, there are days when I wonder if I have anything left to give to anyone else. And then I wake up and do it all over again the next day without acknowledgement from anyone, which is what I mean when I say I am learning how to surrender and serve. Special-needs children require this selfless humility. And if you can't give it, it's very easy to become permanently depressed. The challenge for me moving forward is to feel lucky and blessed by the true joy that comes from serving my special-needs child, Connor Michael, the angel child that's been given to me for a special reason.

Seeking attention is *not* my intent in sharing this story. I have been lead to share the things I am learning from a mentally challenged son who has no idea that what he is teaching me may be the essence of what life was designed to be about—that everything somehow is going to work out and be okay. And that I've been given *the* most beautiful gift; the opportunity to learn how to love, serve, and receive love from a special-needs child who only understands how to give, and isn't waiting for *anything* in return. And to understand that *this* is serene peace.

AND WHO ARE YOU? —A SMALL BACKGROUND IF I MAY

If anyone would have told me that at 49 years of age I'd be writing a book like this, I would have said *"no way, totally impossible."* But I never expected or even thought about the circumstances that were about to come upon me back in the early winter of 2000/2001 when my son Connor was clinically diagnosed with *Williams Syndrome*—a time that will always be *cemented* in my memory as if it happened yesterday.

Born the first of five children, three sisters and one brother, to proud and committed parents, I was brought up in an entrepreneurial family where hard work, self-determination, self-reliance, and dedication were not only important, but the way in which you were supposed to *be* as a person. These attributes were important to nail down, shall we say. Being a self-starter was perhaps most important of all, if you asked my father. Get up, get dressed, have your plan of attack, then *get moving*. I think I was around 7 or 8 years old when he gave me my first full-blown Day-Timer calendar so I could begin learning to manage and prioritize my time. Got the picture? An organized, taskmaster father who believed that accomplishing the task at hand and then moving on to the next one was not only an important lesson, but also the real *core* of how to become successful in life. This bit of information is important since this *pattern* of living, burned into my head since I was a child, would be challenged head-on to its very core when my son was born.

We were by no means financially well off as a family, but we never went without in terms of anything we needed. We didn't take airplanes on family trips, as there were seven of us; it was the wood-paneled Chrysler station wagon loaded down to the max. We had plenty of food, nice clothes, went on summer driving trips to Colorado, Canada, and northern Minnesota, and always had the athletic gear we needed for hockey, tennis, baseball, water and snow skiing, and the other sports we participated in. Looking back, life was good and I felt lucky. Childhood was a good and happy time.

My mother, in addition to being an "at home" mom, also taught French and English at the local middle school a few blocks from our house. Since I can remember, my father was self-employed in the advertising business, so we were used to dinnertime discussions about how things were going; new clients, clients who were leaving the firm, and general concerns about building a small business. We enjoyed family camping and skiing trips, and all of us were competitive athletes. Swimming, baseball, hockey, tennis, water and snow skiing were all part of learning about people—and life.

My father, always the taskmaster of the family, made sure that we chipped in and did our chores on a regular basis whether we wanted to or not, contributing to the family's well-being. Chores often came before homework, practice, or sporting events. We got decent grades in spite of all the major projects around our 110-year-old house on the lake. The house actually had newspaper stuffed in the walls for insulation, as we learned when we began to remodel.

Aside from the typical sibling in fighting, I had a loving, safe, and happy upbringing. I learned that if you wanted to get anywhere in life, you'd better be diligent, work hard, stay focused, and remain upbeat throughout the hills and the valleys of life because they were going to happen (just never to me; for sure, never to me!)

Church was an important part of my upbringing as well, and we went to the local Catholic Church. Between my experience as an alter boy and influences from my aunt, a Carmelite Nun for 45-plus years, I was raised to believe in and revere God.

However, all of the things I would learn in my early years were going to be tested and challenged to their core much later on—in spades. So much so that, at times, I didn't know if I could live by them anymore, or if they were just for other people, but not for me.

Aside from playing competitive hockey, tennis, and baseball since I was a kid, and keeping a B average in school, my first brush with the unexpected came on March 26, 1979 at 5:50 a.m. on an interstate highway headed west for The University of Montana in Missoula. I was returning for spring quarter as a college freshman. My parents let me take the jeep for the semester.

After driving from Minneapolis to just outside Billings, I couldn't stay awake any longer, so I pulled over and asked the person riding with me, who'd been sleeping for several hours, if she felt okay to drive. About 5:30 a.m. we made the switch. Twenty minutes later, she fell asleep behind the wheel and veered off the highway. The jeep rolled end-over-end twice, according to the trucker behind us who witnessed the accident and stopped to help. The force of the impact almost dropped the engine out of the jeep. I was thrown out the back of the vehicle a couple hundred feet. She was pinned in by the roll bar with just a few missing teeth, but went into shock soon after she was helped out, probably after seeing me.

I lay on the highway, my waist and legs on the pavement, my mouth full of blood and gravel, my left hand pointing in the wrong direction, I couldn't move my legs, and I was working hard to get enough air.

With a smashed left wrist and 90 percent compression fractures of lumbar one and two, I had broken my back pretty badly, a half inch from being paralyzed from the waist down according to the doctors in the emergency room. Thankful to be alive, competitive college hockey and tennis were now history. No way would contact sports ever be an option for me again. After being flown back to Minneapolis, I began a three-year recovery process of constant rehab and therapy, wearing a custom-made metal brace from my neck to my waist, which helped me stand and balance as I learned to walk again. The brace was the substitute for Harrington Rods, an option the doctors at Mayo Clinic offered as another avenue of treatment if the steel brace didn't work.

After finishing college around therapy sessions, I got a job with an international nonprofit educational and musical group called Up With People, traveling frequently and securing funds for and promoting large-scale events. Being involved in the half-time entertainment for Super-Bowl XVI at the Pontiac Silverdome in Detroit, and working with senior executives of large firms involved in sponsoring big events was great business experience.

At age 26, a business partner and I started a technology-oriented distributorship serving multinational clients in the banking, credit card collections, outbound telemarketing, and receivables management industries. Years later, we founded a second firm, providing background credential verification services to large employers. Life was getting back on track.

Thirty-one, still single, and caring for my father's mother who had the beginnings of early stage dementia and an enlarged heart, I sold my ownership in both businesses and struck off into the music business. I recorded several tracks at Prince's studio in Minneapolis with the best of musicians, hoping to secure a recording contract with one of the major labels, but to no avail. There was no recording contract, lots of red ink, and a dwindling savings account after two successful ventures. All of a sudden I felt unsuccessful; my first major-league failure.

While putting the pieces back together, I met a woman several years younger with a beautiful 2-year-old daughter. We married a year and a half later, and I started my next venture, a management consultancy launched with the publishing of my first business book. Years later, a second book followed, and a third book was published in 2007.

Managing to grow the business amongst the tumultuous times after the dot-com disaster, the telecommunications and technology slowdown, 9/11, and the financial shenanigans of senior officers at several large firms engaged in fraud, was ultra challenging, to say the least.

In the midst of building a life for my family and me and all the ups and downs that entails, my wife (now ex-wife, I'll explain) announced she was pregnant and that we were going to have a baby in August 1998. Excited and nervous at the same time, the overriding anticipation of our first biological child together was a peaceful thing to think about. The preparation and countdown for a new baby began.

CHAPTER TWO
WHAT MAKES YOU SO SPECIAL?

Absolutely nothing. I'm a proud father who, like many others, works hard to provide for his family so they have what they need throughout life. As an entrepreneur of twenty-some years with all the fits and starts that that life can bring to keep clients happy, the cash flow somewhat stable (as clients file bankruptcy, stiff you, and lift your intellectual property), and build relationships with people who will hopefully remain in their jobs for more than a year or so, I was managing pretty well on all fronts. I've always liked children, so having a biological child was exciting, and made me feel lucky and full of pride. I would work on being the best father I could be and focus on giving my new child and my daughter the kind of upbringing that I had. And of course—if it were a boy, then we would do it all! He'd play hockey, baseball, and tennis, just like his dad. We'd do all the cool stuff that only dads and their sons can do together.

PREPARATIONS FOR HIS COMING—HOPES, DREAMS AND EXPECTATIONS

There was so much to do to get ready! Getting the baby's room painted, crib and mobiles set up, laying out blue and pink blankets—we were all on standby for the big day. As we were preparing, all of these pictures of what I wanted and assumed life would be like with a new child came flooding into my mind—pictures of what I wanted to do with him (if it was a boy), where we'd go together, the things we'd talk about and experience as he grew. I wondered if my thoughts were similar to the pictures and feelings a mother has when she quietly hopes for a girl, so she can do all the special things with her daughter that her mother did with her. Of course, I would have been happy if we'd had a girl. But if it was a boy, we could do it all—and we would. My daughter was so much fun, so active, energetic, and happy, that having a son with the same attributes would make us the complete family I had always envisioned. One beautiful and talented little girl and a new baby boy. Maybe.

I didn't understand where all these thoughts and expectations were coming from, but they were clearly in the forefront of my mind. As if I was in charge of the whole thing from the moment my child was born until he or she got married. No doubt about it: we were going to do *all* the things I had dreamed about with my new child as if I could paint on a canvas just exactly how things were going to go from day one. I had it all planned out. It was like candy being offered to a child, as if I could reach out and select *just those pieces* that I wanted for my child and me. Looking back now, I can say how unbelievably *selfish* I was in preparing for my child's coming, by focusing on what he would do with his daddy, and what he would someday become.

And nowhere in this maze of exciting expectations was there any picture, any thought, or any doubt that we'd have anything but a healthy, happy, and *normal* child. Nowhere! The thought never entered my mind. Hopes, dreams, and expectations are so important in helping us to keep pushing forward in life. But these very same pictures can also create lots of anger, sadness, and feelings of utter hopelessness and despair as they did for me, when the expectations so firmly in your head are or will never be realized—ever. I was about to learn this lesson firsthand and suffer the deep sorrow that comes and goes as a result. A host of emotions, anger, disappointments and frustrations that I would need to learn how to handle and deal with forever, moving forward.

I can't speak for anyone else. But to act as I did, as if I was in charge of the entire event—from birth throughout my child's life—was a harsh awakening that someone else was in charge of the whole thing, though I thought my hands were firmly on the wheel and that I was driving the bus! I think it's a classic flaw of sorts with an entrepreneur type.

What I couldn't understand at the time was that I was setting myself up for a feeling of hopelessness and despair so deep, that I didn't know if I could ever climb out of it.

THE PERFECT SON—WE WILL NAME HIM CONNOR MICHAEL

I stood at the side of the bed next to my wife like the dutiful husband, holding her hand and keeping a cold cloth on her forehead as the doctor and nurses swirled around her bedside debating whether an epidural was necessary; everything was moving so fast.

The hospital room was buzzing with medical staff barking directives rapid fire as I attempted to keep her calm and comfortable. I was actually panicked. I had never gone through anything like this before. This was our first biological child together and everything was new to me.

I wanted to update my mom so I peeked out the hospital room door, finding her in the hall. I told her what was going on and that it might be a while before the baby was ready to come. Being a spiritually connected woman, she walked down the hall and began to pray, as she typically does in times of great need. Within ten minutes the baby was ready to come. The doctor and nurses were amazed and I was freaked out, and nervous, and feeling in the way.

Then, all of a sudden, the baby started to come. There was no crying, as I remember. A quiet baby, and a boy! Six pounds six ounces. They scurried him off to a corner of the room pretty quickly to be cleaned and checked over because the cord was wrapped around his neck. After he was all cleaned and put in a blanket, they presented him to us to hold. The most precious gift I have ever been given. I stared in homage at my firstborn son and held him as gently as I knew how. I couldn't hold in my tears. I had *never* felt this way before. I couldn't speak. He was so peaceful.

We had picked out a strong Irish name as a symbol for the strong boy I knew he'd become, Connor Michael. I was overcome with a deep sense of peace as I made the sign of the cross on his forehead. He was a *blessed* boy now, though he was yet to be baptized by Father Arnold. It was all so amazing and spiritual. I stood straight as a tree, holding my new son and feeling that now, more than ever, I would be an even better provider as he was going to be denied nothing in life.

When we brought him home from the hospital, the normalness of a busy home life with a newborn began, probably not any different from anyone else's crazed life with a new baby. But early on we noticed a major intolerance to milk and lots of crying, different from how calm and relatively quiet he seemed in the hospital. But then again, he was just a baby, so this was all normal, right? Nothing to sweat or worry about. I had a new son, and this was just life with a newborn.

But the crying continued. Lots of crying. As I recall, my wife felt the crying might be a little more than normal, and so did I. Plus, he wasn't eating very much. At seven months old, he still hadn't gained much weight, and after numerous doctors visits (and what looked like a large "outy" belly button), it was determined that Connor needed a triple hernia operation. The doctors seemed to agree that maybe the reason he was colicky and in so much pain was because of the little hole under his navel. As he breathed we could see his intestines moving underneath his belly button. That *must* have been hurting him so it needed to be addressed.

The doctor at Children's Hospital did an amazing job on the surgery, though I was a nervous wreck during the procedure. To see our 7-month-old in the recovery room in his little hospital bed, all bundled up in a blanket with an IV in his arm made me feel helpless again. But with a successful operation, we anticipated he would begin to eat more over time and finally start gaining some weight. (His head seemed pretty small.) I felt relieved that maybe things would get better— that he would start eating more, have less gastrointestinal problems, and maybe the crying would lessen when we brought him home from the hospital.

But this was not to be. The crying continued. We bought the most expensive baby milk on the planet (something like $5 a can!), which I purchased by the caseload. It seemed to be the only kind of milk that Connor could digest. This helped some, but he still wasn't gaining much weight. We decided to take him to see additional pediatricians and specialists who all ended up saying about the same thing: Not to worry, he's just got some type of bad acid reflux. They told us to cool it on the milk and other diary products.

The advice was hardly comforting because he was clearly still in pain. We were starting to wonder if anyone could help us find any answers so he could be comfortable. We were exhausted, maybe a bit on edge, and my wife needed a break. I suggested she go to Scottsdale with my sisters to get some rest and relax in the sun.

I took the week off from work so I could stay home with Connor because I didn't trust anyone to watch him other than my wife. It was just Connor and me, all day and all night, for what I recall was about six days. And *then* I understood. I understood how uncomfortable he really was. How much he cried. How I got no sleep. How he'd spit food right back at me when I'd be feeding him. How he'd try to smell anything and everything before it entered his mouth and if the texture of the food didn't seem right to him, or if it entered his mouth the wrong way or whatever, I'd get it right back. And how he'd wake up in the middle of the night several times to cry… and cry… and cry. It hurt so much to hold him as he cried, knowing it seemed like there was nothing I could do other than rock him back and forth in my arms, gently rubbing his head. I was beginning to wonder if I could handle it. It was never-ending.

The stress and constant worrying was getting intense. Even though I was trying to keep calm, gentle, and loving, we were getting no real answers as to why he was so uncomfortable. None! And we were going to very good doctors. I worried nonstop, which was not my nature. It was not the way I was raised to be. Maybe some men can handle this level of stress without any problem, but I was beginning to have difficulty and I knew it. I was consumed with so much doubt and fear that I couldn't focus on *anything* except Connor. I began to view my work as an inconvenient hassle, though I definitely needed the income. And I had a hard time keeping my emotions from spilling over into decisions I needed to make to keep the business moving forward. We were living in America with the supposed best health care system, but it wasn't working very well for our son.

There were days while my wife was deservedly relaxing with my sisters in Arizona that I didn't get out of my pajamas. I held Connor constantly, rocking him back and forth. His discomfort continued and my stress level continued to rise, as it seemed nothing I did brought him any comfort. I felt helpless and hopeless, as if we were on some deserted island with all the medical experts saying, *"Gee, I'm sorry, but we don't feel there is really anything that out of the ordinary with your son, though we understand that he's very uncomfortable."* My wife and I believed differently. He was in more pain than seemed necessary and we were not going to stop searching for ways to help our boy, until we found something that helped.

The days became longer, lonelier, and we became more isolated, not seeing our friends nearly like we used to because there just didn't seem to be the time to really enjoy them. Being consumed with Connor made it hard to focus on anything else. Besides, we probably weren't that much *fun* to be around either. I can only speak for myself, but I was wound pretty tight, worrying about my son all the time. Perhaps others felt we were too *heavy* to be around or that we couldn't really relax or loosen up, which was probably correct, but sad when you think about it. And though I'd begun to hear that these kinds of family situations and stresses could take a toll on any marriage, it had yet to occur to me that our marriage and personal relationship was becoming an unspoken series of deep sadness, fear, and hopelessness. There wasn't much laughter in the house any more as I recall—no joking, and not many smiles. Except for my daughter's enlightening presence, love, energy, and continued accomplishments in the classroom and on the basketball court, life was becoming an unexciting, serious, never-ending grind.

I felt like my head was locked in a vice-grip cranked as tight as it could possibly go. Nothing made me smile. The worry never let up. And for a guy who'd been raised to have a positive outlook on life, I couldn't see *anything* positive ahead. My mind was in a thick fog and I had no idea if it would lift anytime soon. I had never envisioned that life could be this hard. Never! My personality was beginning to change to that of an introvert bracing for the next round of bad news about our son. *Maybe I should just stay in my foxhole*, I thought. There's only so much one can take, right? The perfect son? Yes. He was our beautiful little boy. But he was in so much pain and there was nothing I could do. And *that* was not the perfect little situation for our boy.

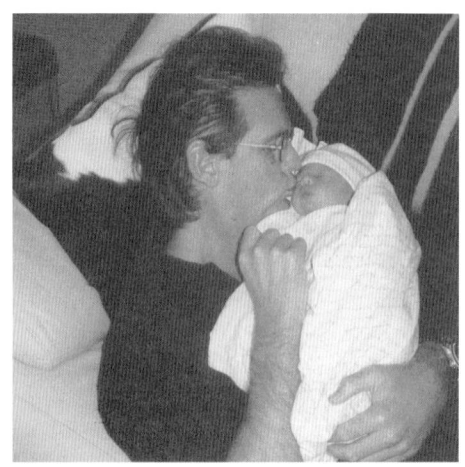

Above: A few days old

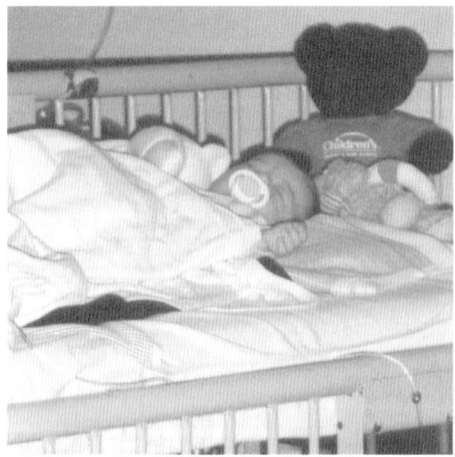

Above and below: Triple hernia surgery at the hospital

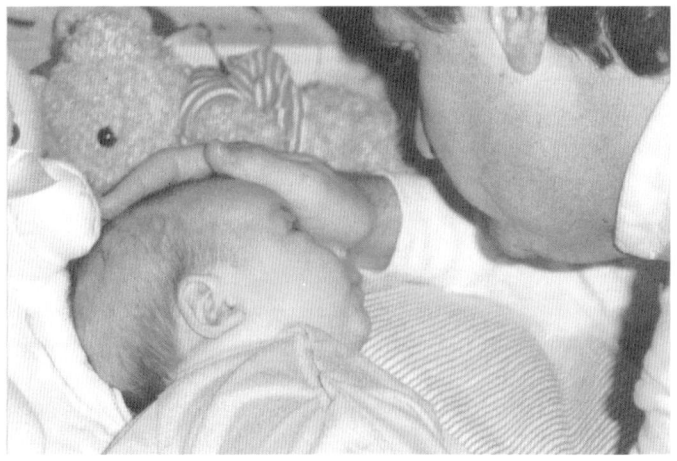

HE'S NOT TRACKING, IS HE?

Lots of people have a common way of describing situations by putting them into two basic buckets. Maybe you do the same thing. People say you're either *on track* or *not on track*. Those who aren't on track are usually working hard to get back there. And while we all like to simplify situations to this extreme, as if it's that easy to get back on track at will, I was definitely not on track, nor was our son—and we knew it. My career also seemed way off track, like it was sliding right through my hands. My head was so heavy and out of focus on the deals I needed to close. Everything seemed totally upside down, with one of the two most important people in our lives suffering constantly and we were right there with him, suffering and searching for answers and help, but none was really coming. There appeared to be no relief in sight, though we tried to keep a good "game face" on as we pressed ahead. I attempted to put a hopeful spin on our attitude toward life and the circumstances in front of us, since we were fighters. But the *fight* was getting old and very tiring. There wasn't much gas left in my tank.

After Connor's first birthday, we intensified the doctor visits, becoming even more proactive with the medical community. We asked more questions—to the point of being a pain in the rump to the doctors and specialists. But frankly, we didn't care. This was our son. We listened to every shred of medical advice we got about what other things might be medically wrong with Connor Michael. Deep down we felt he wasn't tracking, but we never really talked about it that much during our alone time, which was almost nonexistent (except for talking about it to and from doctor visits). It was almost too painful to discuss, though we both seemed to know or anticipate what the other was thinking. It was a hollow sadness as black as a bottomless pit—a silent fear that it could be something serious, though we tried to remain positive as though the next day would bring news of possible answers. Something would come, we kept telling ourselves, and it was *just* around the corner.

Hope was all we had. But to be honest, even being hopeful was a tall order for me. Like I said, my parents and grandparents taught me to be positive and never lose hope. This was ingrained in me since I was a boy, so I knew how important it was to look on the bright side of things. But *Mr. Positive* was becoming *Mr. Full-of-Doubt.* I couldn't smile if you promised me a thousand dollars. It wasn't in me. I couldn't find one. I was filled with sadness. It wouldn't go away, and I couldn't stop worrying. I felt like a walking zombie. I couldn't focus on my work, my wife, or even our daughter in the way she deserved with all of her activities—just on Connor. *That* was the proper focus, I thought, even as my business began to slide, as did thousands of others nationwide that were having *major* problems after the dot.com disaster and the attack on the World Trade Center, which caused thousands of companies to shut off spending and go into a foxhole and wait.

Almost overnight, corporations froze spending on *anything* that was even remotely related to sales and management training and strategic consulting, the field I'd been in for several years. But even *that* wasn't nearly as important as my son. I almost didn't care about anything except the health and welfare of my son and daughter. And right now, my son came first, damn it! So why couldn't clients cut me some slack? Couldn't they show me a little compassion and understanding in a family related matter? Or *at the end of the day,* as clients love to say, is it ALL just about the dollar? It sure seemed like it, because the empathy wasn't there; lots of glowing verbal comments, but nothing to back it up.

Who was it that said that in times of great struggle, you learn who your *real* friends are? And whom you can count on in times of great need? Anyway, this helped fuel my feelings that we were really all alone.

I would get up in the middle of the night, go downstairs and cry so I wouldn't wake up my wife. The sadness was thick, deep, and heavy. Our relationship was dying and I think we both knew it, though it wasn't discussed much (to my memory) other than comments or short bursts that we needed some counseling or something, which neither of us seemed to do anything about. We were just too busy and so focused on Connor.

We were like platonic college roommates. No time to concentrate on each other's needs or wants because we were both focused on Connor. And I was certifiably sick and tired of hearing people tell me in their ever so soft, even-tempered, calm voices with their tender puppy-dog looks, as their heads would cock to the left, *"You know, God never gives you more than you can handle."* That statement was total bullshit, in my opinion, because he'd just given us that in spades! And God? Where the HELL was *he* is this whole thing? That was a great question for which I had no answer. I felt totally abandoned, though I'd been raised to believe in the almighty creator, and was an altar boy to boot. But why in the heck had he given me such a crumby life of pain, never-ending fear, doubt, and hardship? It was more than a little hard to be a trusting and loyal believer when all this constant hardship had become my life! Perhaps I was being punished. It sure felt like it—and for what?

I had absolutely no flipping idea how I was going handle it! I felt stranded and totally alone! I think we both did. Not to mention, I couldn't focus correctly on my corporate clients and their nonstop demands. It felt as though they were badgering me, though I know they were just being clients. I wasn't designed to handle this. Didn't the *man upstairs* know this? It felt like I was coming apart because nothing was making any sense to me and *nothing* was on track. And for a type A guy into having things in order, this was not a good thing.

Life wasn't supposed to be like this. I knew of nobody that was going through these kinds of hardships. I was tired of trying so hard to bring things back on track because nothing I was doing for our son, or for our life, seemed like it was working. Things were so old, so hard, and such a grind all the time. People would say, *"He's just not the same guy any more, you know? — Everything is always so heavy with him—don't you think? It's like he just can't loosen up."* That was hard to hear. But the truth is, there are many people in this world who really aren't interested in helping. You learn this when your life seems to be in shambles. There are few who really lend a hand.

The medical tests being recommended to us seemed more and more elaborate as we pushed on for answers; an EEG (an electroencephalogram—a brain scan), an EKG (an electrocardiogram—a quick glimpse of the heart waves), more and different kinds of blood tests, as well as additional meetings with his everyday doctors, and gastrointestinal professionals advising different types of foods, various specialists looking beyond gastrointestinal issues, and on, and on, and on.

Have you ever been in the waiting room of a hospital or specialist's office in the middle of the day (after filling out the insurance forms, which can make you feel as though they're going to take your house if they don't get their money)? It's not a good feeling; all alone, while the rest of the world is out working away and getting ahead in their lives while you are at the mercy of some doctors, who are, of course going to do their best, but are also very BUSY. They've got others they need to see right behind you. It tends to make you feel a bit helpless at times, and off track.

And while all these professionals were attempting to be reassuring, it seemed they too were perplexed and tentative, as if they weren't telling us everything they thought. But we were probably paranoid because we were desperate for answers. We picked up on their unspoken concerns but it was still too hard to discuss between us. My growing fear was that nobody would be able to tell us anything to help our son. And he *still* wasn't tracking.

I could see the sadness in my wife's eyes, a depth of loneliness that isn't cured with *date night*. As the man of the house, I did my best to hide the same fear. We were tired, I was scared, and our son was hurting. No one seemed to know what was going on. How could it be that some of the best medical doctors around couldn't figure out what was going on with our son? They were the experts. It didn't make any sense to me, and as a result, I was becoming withdrawn. I think my wife was too. We were all by ourselves on this one. Not fair. Not fair at all.

Little did we know that the pediatric neurologist we'd seen a year or so earlier had a hunch about Connor, but it was never shared with us. Evidently, he had ordered a specific blood test called *The Fish Test* that was never performed by the lab. Somehow there was a screw-up and the test was never done. We found this out a good while later.

What we did understand was sadness—deep, long, and unending. *How much of this were we supposed to take?* I would ask in my prayers. *I want some answers, damn it! Talk to me! Is this going to be our life?* Searching for medical answers hadn't told us anything so far. I wondered if we were in for a lifetime of uncertainty while we put on a *happy face* for the rest of the world, which only wanted to talk about happy things. Our life was not happy. It was a grind, steel-on-steel with no end in sight.

The volume of correspondence between doctors, specialists, hospitals, the health-care provider and others grew by the month. Being the organized one––or so I thought—I began a card file and filing system to keep things straight. It was a project worthy of outsourcing with all the moving parts. Which doctors are where, which ones have moved to other hospitals and clinics, who said what, when, etc., and the continual changes from the insurance provider regarding who was in-network versus out-of-network, what they did and didn't cover, which changed frequently. I didn't go to college for this, but a semester could easily be designed for all of this bunk—a task to keep as current as possible for our boy. We were not going to give up—no way. That was not in my nature, though the thought had crossed my mind more than a few times.

I couldn't remember the last time my wife and I went out for a quiet dinner or just a walk in the neighborhood. What was *that* like? And it felt as though we'd never do it again. And romance? Forget it. It was the last thing on my mind actually, hers probably too, based on the total lack of touching and intimacy between us. It felt like the last time we'd even kissed—I mean really kissed—was years. I wish I were exaggerating, but for us, this was our life.

Some of my buddies would joke around when we were in private calling me, "Mr. Once a Semester." They thought it was hilarious, yet it wasn't funny to me. It reminded me all the more of how far off center life had become. You could have put a one-foot square wooden beam down the center of our bed and neither one of us would have gotten any slivers. Intimacy was a distant memory as we hunkered down for another long and cold Minnesota winter of no answers, not knowing how to help our son. Maybe we would hold hands— maybe, in the car on the way to the next doctors appointment, with Connor quietly in the back seat all strapped in, his soft, gentle little face staring out the window sensing where mommy and daddy where taking him next. It seemed like he was starting to learn where we were going. Another doctor, another hospital, another specialist, test, or analysis. When were we going to learn something conclusive about our beautiful little child?

DUMPTY
THE
AND
COULDN'T
AGAIN!

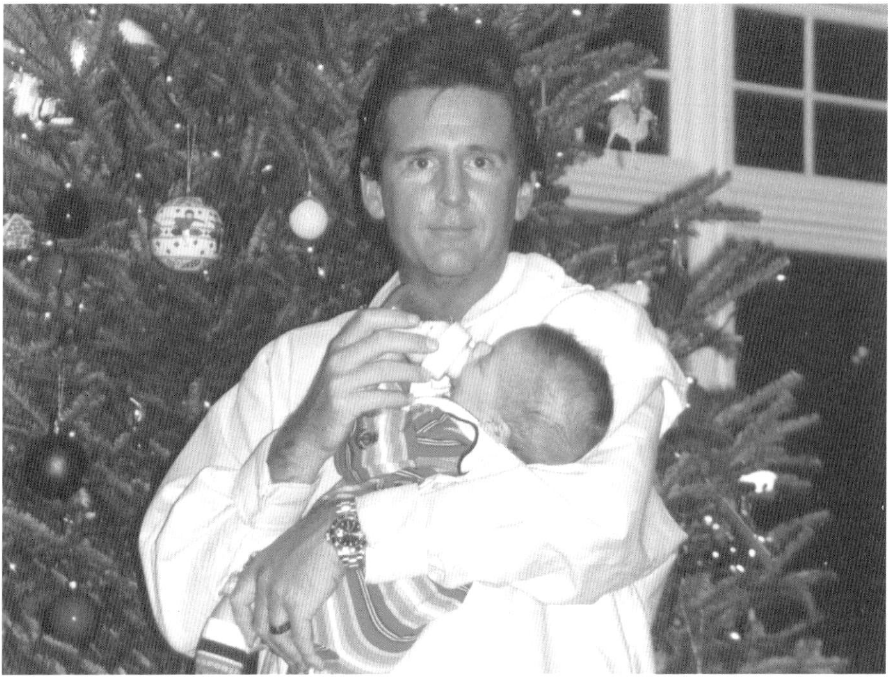

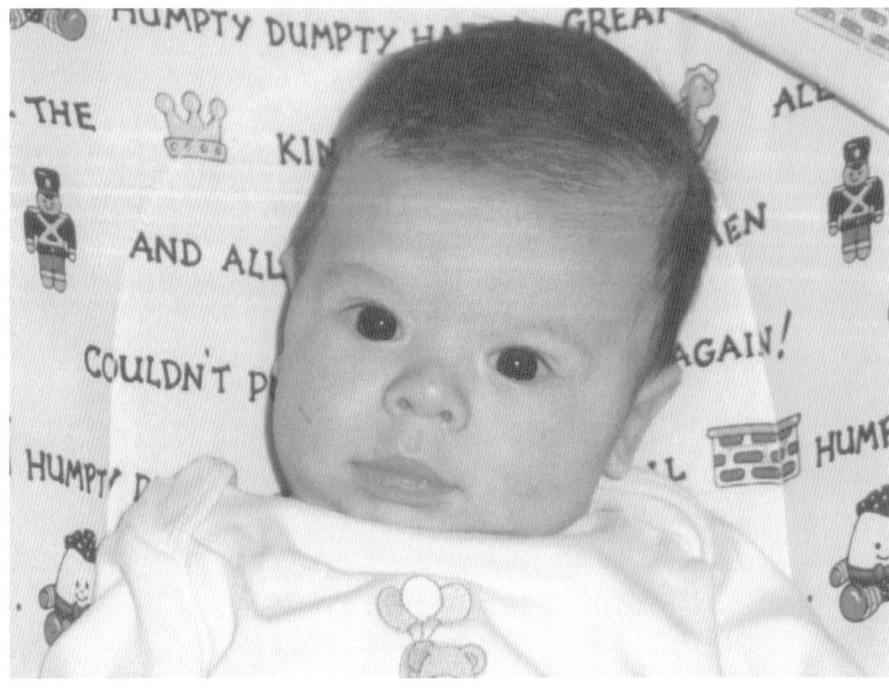

31

With more time with doctors and still no answers, we went along with all the continued tests being recommended, hoping they'd reveal something. We'd done all the things they'd suggested, but still nothing—except more tentativeness from the medical professionals. My level of confidence in doctors was dropping like a rock. I didn't understand how the "experts" couldn't figure things out. *What's the benefit to keep doing all these tests*, I would ask, *and then get back this look from the doctors as if we were total irritants because of the litany of questions we were asking?* But they were tentative and couldn't hide it. They too were confused, and this made us feel all the more nervous and alone.

There was one test we had yet to do because, as I recall, no one had yet brought it to our attention—an echocardiogram, an ultrasound of Connor's heart. It shows the blood flow of the heart. I didn't understand the relevance of the test, but if it could shed some light on things, we were all for it. So we said yes and scheduled the test.

We booked the appointment to have the procedure done at Children's Heart Clinic, one of the finest in the Twin Cities. The highly regarded doctor scheduled to see us happened to be the co-founder of the clinic, an amazingly kind and compassionate man.

It was late fall of 2000 with another Minnesota winter just around the corner. Connor had just turned two a couple of months earlier. The day was cloudy and brisk—a day burned into my memory as if it happened just yesterday. The highway was bone dry, cold and windy. It felt like the first snow was not far off, just quiet and still, with no one on the road; a day reserved just for us.

We got Connor all bundled up and I loaded him into the back seat of our SUV, getting him all strapped in and comfy with Snuffy, his purple blanky, as we drove to Children's Hospital and Heart Clinic for the procedure. Like every other trip to various doctors' offices, I don't recall us talking much, if at all, as we drove downtown to the clinic. Like so many other times, it just seemed easier not to talk, as all the possible scenarios went swirling around in my (and probably my wife's) head about what might be coming next.

I remember how cold and gray it was that day. As we got closer to the hospital, Connor seemed to sense where we were going and started to get nervous. His face just had this look. Every time we'd bundle him up and put him in the car he'd clutch me so tight as if to be telling me, *"Daddy, hold me,"* as he dug his fingernails into the side of my neck like he didn't want me to let him go.

After the routine sign-in process with the myriad of insurance forms, which needed to be filled out each and every time as if they'd never seen you before, we were lead back to one of the waiting rooms with lots of children's toys and told the doctor would be with us shortly. We grabbed some toys to keep Connor occupied and distracted from where we were, though based on the look on his face; he seemed to know where he was. We'd been to *so* many doctors and specialists, but we sat patiently waiting. We held Connor and the toy, which seemed to occupy his attention for all but a few seconds.

A sharp knock on the door broke the nervousness and the doctor came in, a warm, kind, interested, friendly man. After the introductions and niceties he sat down, grabbed his clipboard, stared at Connor intensely, then looked at me, back at Connor, then back at me, and within a few seconds his entire demeanor seemed to change. People say that in times of trauma, people who experience the very same event will recall it, or describe it differently—or take away a totally different memory of what actually happened though they went through the same thing. Therefore, I don't know how my wife would recall things. But this is what I remember from that day, which replays itself over and over in my mind.

"Question to you, Michael. Does Connor look like you—or does he look like your wife?" The way in which he asked the question, quick and direct, made me a tad nervous.

"I don't know really," I responded.

"Let me ask again," I recall him saying in an even more firm and direct tone. "Does your son look like you—or your wife?"

"I don't know. I guess me, but he also has some of my wife's features too. He's only two," I said.

The doctor became more intense, but maintained a professional demeanor. He asked some additional questions related to other tests, and other doctors we'd seen, and then said something to the effect of, "Look at Connor's forehead. Look at his lips. Do you see the elfin features in his face? I think Connor might have WILLIAMS SYNDROME. Have the other doctors not seen this? Just a minute. I will be right back. I want you to read something in a medical journal. Be right back!"

He left the room quickly and I was totally numb. *He has what? What is Williams Syndrome?* Everything stopped. The room was spinning or maybe it was just my head. I began to cry. I don't remember what my wife was doing. My mind was racing a hundred miles an hour. We had never heard of *Williams Syndrome*. No one had ever brought it up. What was Williams Syndrome? It sounded serious based on his tone and the way in which his demeanor changed so quickly. I'm sure he was being as professional as he knew how, though it appeared he was surprised as well. Waiting a few minutes seemed like hours as I grabbed a box of nearby Kleenex® to dry my eyes.

The doctor reappeared with a thick medical journal opened to the place he wanted us to look, asked us to read the page, then left the room again to prepare for Connor's echocardiogram. I held the book open staring at a bunch of words as tears dripped onto the pages blurring my ability to make anything out. *My son has something called what? This is my son! And he has what? Is this permanent?* I couldn't hear anyone talking to me because nobody was talking to me—just my mind asking a million questions all at once!

I stared at the heading **WILLIAMS SYNDROME** but couldn't read. I just stared and sobbed. I don't remember what my wife was doing. But I recall staring at Connor as he sat quietly on the floor playing with some toys, oblivious to what was going on in the room. Just peaceful and content, as if everything was going to be just fine, while Mommy and Daddy were struggling to understand the magnitude of what they'd just been told by a world-renowned specialist who was trying his best to be calm, compassionate, and professional—all things he was doing well, as I remember.

The doctor returned a few minutes later and was gentle as he explained what Williams Syndrome was, and that there were some signs that indicated, at least to him, that Connor might have Williams Syndrome. We both sat there glued to what he was telling us, as if it was so surreal that it just couldn't be happening. The slow-motion movie of our life was beginning and *we* were the principal actors.

"Has Connor had a brain scan—an EEG?" the doctor asked.

"Yes, I believe he has," I said.

"Who did the test? Where was the test done?" I recall him asking. As we struggled to answer, he barked out another question. "Has the Fish Test—The Fish blood work test, has that been done?"

"We don't know, I don't think so, but I don't know," I responded. "He's had lots of blood work, but I don't know if he's had the Fish Test."

"And who did the brain scan?" the doctor asked. When we responded, he acknowledged that the doctor who did that test was good.

I couldn't be polite any longer. "What is Williams Syndrome?" I barked. "What does this mean? What is going on? What does Williams Syndrome have to do with the procedure we're about to do?"

The doctor became fatherly and began explaining in terms we could understand, as we sat there trying to keep our eyes clear of tears.

"Now I am not saying conclusively that Connor has Williams, but he seems to have some of the symptoms and attributes of a child with this very rare condition, in my opinion. Basically, if Connor has Williams Syndrome, he could be missing between 20 and 24 or so genes around chromosome number seven. And this gene deletion or inversion, as it is sometimes called, impacts Connor's cognitive growth and general abilities, his emotions, his fine and gross motor skills, potentially his heart which we might see shortly with the echocardiogram, and many other areas such as gastrointestinal issues, etc. Children with Williams often have elfin features like Connor has. Some in the medical community who have heard of Williams refer to it as having some similar traits to children on the autism spectrum, or mentally retarded or challenged. Williams is very rare, discovered around 1997, I believe. The Fish Test is the specific blood test that we know of that helps confirm the diagnosis, which is why he should have the test. And when we do the echocardiogram shortly, if Connor has aortic stenosis, which is a narrowing of his aorta, this is another symptom that would also point to the probability that Connor might have Williams Syndrome."

I probably don't have the correct order or the exact words as to how the doctor shared the information since I was in a trance when he was speaking, but this is what I remember. The conversation was moving way too fast for me and all I could focus on were two words; MENTALLY RETARDED. He was saying that my son was mentally challenged, and this meant *forever*. Forever! I couldn't get my head around that concept.

The doctor continued on, as I recall. "Typically, many children with Williams will have a narrowing of their aorta coming off the heart, causing the heart to work harder than it should have to, to pump the blood through this narrower passageway. The echo procedure should be able to show us if Connor has aortic stenosis, which would need to be corrected—if pronounced enough—with open-heart surgery at the appropriate time. Again, I'm not saying conclusively that Connor has Williams, but I have seen a few other children with Williams and it's my hunch that he may have it. I will advise you to go and see a world-renowned doctor at the University of Minnesota after we do the Fish Test and know what that tells us. I believe he will be able to give us a more conclusive diagnosis of Connor since he's renown for studying syndromes of the head and neck in children. I need to get prepped for the procedure now. The two of you can stand on either side of Connor as we lay him down on the table to do the echo."

The doctor left the room as we sat in silence, staring at Connor for what seemed like hours. Some nurses appeared to give Connor a liquid sedative to drink, and the doctor reappeared and said it was time. I picked Connor up and carried him down the hall to the room where the nurses and doctor were waiting. My wife and I tried to calm Connor as we laid him on the cold, hard table in this dark corner room as they hooked up the various electrode-looking round rubber pads on Connor's chest. He gripped my hand while trying to pull off the rubber pads as fast as they put them on his chest. Eventually, we were able to get them attached and the test began, Connor fixated on a Teletubbies video on the monitor above.

The room was dark and quiet as they began the test, our eyes fixed on the monitor that showed Connor's heart pumping. As the doctor and nurses talked back and forth, we listened intently to see if we could understand anything they were saying.

"Mommy and Daddy are right here Connor," I whispered. "It's okay, Connor. We're almost done. Just a little bit longer honey." We stared at the monitor waiting to hear the doctor say if he had aortic stenosis.

Images flashed by so fast that we didn't know what we were looking at, or what to look for. We remained silent waiting for the doctor to tell us something as Connor kept saying, *"All done? All done?"*

We stood silently, hovering over our son, waiting for a sign from the doctor. And then it came. He looked at us and said; "See this area here on the monitor?" pointing at the screen. "This is where the narrowing is in Connor's aorta; something that can be corrected with routine open-heart surgery at some point. We will need to keep a close eye on Connor as he grows, his weight and other things. Probably once a year, I will need to see him to monitor the situation to determine if and when we'll need to correct it with open-heart surgery."

"So does he have Williams Syndrome?" I asked.

"I cannot give a conclusive diagnosis at this time, which is why we should send all the medical records over to the doctor at the University. You two should go see him to confirm the diagnosis after we run the Fish Test. But more than likely, he may have Williams. Let's finish the echo and talk more in the other room."

Routine? Open-heart surgery is routine? Are they nuts? Open-heart surgery is *not* routine. Not in my book! I rubbed Connor's hand as they slowly took the rubber pads off his chest, wishing that someone would comfort me. I was numb. We put Connor's clothes on, picked him up, and carried him back down the hall to the room where we began. The doctor came back in.

"Here's what I think we should do. We need to schedule the Fish Test, which will give us more information in regard to whether Connor has Williams. You can schedule the test here at the hospital. After the blood work is back, I will review it with the neurologist who saw Connor, and we'll talk again at that time. And if the blood work indicates he might have Williams, I would advise you to see this world-renowned doctor at the University of Minnesota I mentioned earlier. I know him. He is a retired orthodontist but has been studying syndromes of the head and neck in children for years and is published extensively on the subject. I feel he could help us in diagnosing Connor based on what the blood work looks like, okay? Let's schedule the Fish Test and I will call you after the neurologist and I review it, and we can determine if we should send the files over to the University for another opinion."

Everything the doctor said came into my mind in slow motion as we tried to keep Connor patient. We shook hands, walked down the hall, scheduled the blood test, and walked to the parking garage without saying a word to each other, as I remember. It was surreal. I lifted Connor into our SUV, strapped him in, paid the parking ticket, and drove home feeling as if we were now in some very sad movie. I don't recall looking at my wife as we drove home, just the road. It was *so* cold outside, dry, quiet, and still. When we got home, I don't think we told anyone the news, not even our daughter. We had dinner, gave Connor his bath, which usually calmed him down, and my wife worked with my daughter on her homework or something after Connor went down.

I remember sitting on the bed in our master bedroom, starring at the wall feeling numb and hopeless, as if all the wind had gone out of my sails and the ocean was still. If I tried to be optimistic and comforting for my wife that night, I don't remember it. Everything was moving in slow motion with all those *pictures* of *my perfect life* with our son flashing through my mind in warp speed––almost too much to bear. My mind was being tortured.

My wife and I didn't speak when she came into the bedroom. We stared at the wall attempting to digest what we had just heard. I would *never* forget this day. This was not supposed to happen to me, not to Connor, not to our family, and not to us. The spiral was beginning. I was in a trance, as if we were all alone on some island with no compass and no clear path to follow. No life raft, no one to help us or hold us. I didn't know what to do, and I couldn't turn off the tape in my mind that kept playing over and over again, *"Your son has Williams Syndrome! Have the other doctors missed this?"*

Connor got up the next day and I couldn't focus on anything. I might have taken the day off from work, I don't remember. Or maybe it was the weekend. I just wanted to be with him, to hold him, look at him, put my cheek next to his and feel his warmth. I had to be with him. He seemed so peaceful and content without a care in the world. No fear, just a peace that Mommy and Daddy were going to take care of him. But I needed someone to take care of me, and tell me that somehow, everything would be okay; that Connor's future and our family would be okay, that our marriage would endure. And that our LIFE was going to be okay! But no one was there to do that, and we didn't know how to help each other. My wife was probably trying to cope with the news as best she could, though I was too slammed to ask. All of a sudden, Mr. Positive, Mr. Can-do, Mr. Take-Charge, couldn't see a path forward because there was no path, just a thick fog and a feeling that we were sinking into quicksand. Not a good thing for a self-employed entrepreneur that's supposed to have a happy face on when meeting potential clients! I didn't think I could do that any more. I felt overwhelmed, filled with sadness, and fear.

I don't remember when we told our parents the news, but I remember *all the questions* coming back from them and my brother and sisters, for which we had no real answers yet, because we didn't know either; nor did the doctors, really. *Everybody* wanted detailed specifics, timelines, how severe Williams was in comparison to things like Down Syndrome, Autism, Tourette Syndrome, and mental retardation. *Exactly what was Williams Syndrome? How long would it last? Would he ever outgrow it or was it forever? What does his lifespan look like? How much extra outside help would Connor require throughout his life? Would or could he ever get married, have children, drive a car or live on his own? Would he for sure need open-heart surgery, and if so, when? What would the surgery accomplish? How did this happen anyway? Was this a genetic fluke or did my wife or I have some gene or abnormality that we passed onto Con-*

nor? Is Williams some new discovery in the medical community, because we've never heard of it? Just exactly where does he fall on the Williams scale of severity? —And on and on and on. The more questions, the deeper I sank into total despair because we didn't have any answers. All the questions kept forcing the tape in my mind to play back, *"Your son has Williams Syndrome. He is mentally retarded."*

All of these questions plus tons more were the same ones we were asking the doctors. Unfortunately, we didn't have any answers yet, often because they didn't know for certain either. We were in uncharted territory, which made me feel hopeless, almost like I was being punished. This wasn't supposed to happen to me. Not Mr. Full-of-Hope. My life was supposed to be happy, fun, and successful—meeting exciting people, traveling to new places with our family and living a normal life, whatever that is. But these things were sliding away, as if I didn't deserve them any more, replaced with a deep coating of life stress and pressure surrounding my first-born son and what seemed a permanent medical diagnosis we'd have to learn about, understand, and manage to live with for the rest of our lives as best we could.

At Sunday mass, I held Connor as if it were the last time I'd have him in my arms. My head felt like it weighed 200 pounds as I knelt in the church pew asking God for a sign that things were going to be all right somehow. I wanted to know what was to be gained in all of the sorrow and shock. But nothing came. I wasn't getting anything back. Ever felt like God has turned on you? That you've gotten a raw deal or the shaft? That he's not listening? That you're all by yourself? I had no comfort, just a cold feeling about having to find the answers on my own. This didn't track with what I'd learned about faith, grace, and patience growing up in the church.

December 2000 brought us a quiet and lonely Christmas. It was just family, as we didn't feel like going to holiday parties. I don't recall celebrating with friends, or even shopping for gifts. I think we ordered most of them from catalogs that year. We put the tree up though I don't know why, because it didn't feel like there was anything to celebrate. Everything was hollow, cold, quiet, and lonely.

After Christmas and New Year's Day, it was back to the grind. I was trying to be positive at work but not doing a good job of it. We waited for the results of the blood work, grasping for a sliver of hope that maybe the doctor was off his rocker and didn't have a clue about what he was talking about. *Maybe he was totally off base and Connor didn't have Williams Syndrome.* I tried to hang onto these thoughts, but they never lasted for more than a few minutes, as I was becoming an accomplished pessimist. I knew the doctors we'd been seeing were top notch, and the likelihood of them being way off was remote.

Sometime in the new year, the hospital called to say the results of the blood work were in. We booked another appointment to talk with the doctor about what the results from the Fish Test showed. On the day we drove to the clinic I was attempting to be hopeful. As I put Connor in the back seat and strapped him in with Snuffy, (which he likes to talk to), he had this look of total serenity on his face. A calmness that Mommy and Daddy *knew* what they were doing, that we *knew* how to care for him, that we'd be there no matter what. It was a total peace, trust, and calmness that pierced through me and made me cry. I made the sign of the cross on his forehead, getting him all situated in his car seat. He loved sitting in the Navigator like King Tutt, looking at everything as we drove downtown again, hopefully to hear good news—a development—something to hope for instead of what we were expecting to hear.

My wife's hand was cold and limp as I reached out to hold it in a gesture that everything would somehow be okay, while my mind raced with scenarios of life moving forward. I put on some classical music, which always seemed to calm Connor as we drove to the place we'd become all too familiar with, Children's Hospital and Heart Clinic, on another wintry Minnesota day.

The mind is a powerful thing. So powerful that when you get bad news, news you don't want to hear, it can block you from consciously remembering specifics because it's just too hard. I can't honestly tell you how the doctor told us the news, or, the exact words he used. Just that the blood work was positive indicating that Connor more than likely *did* have Williams Syndrome—the *gene deletion* around chromosome seven, and that we should forward all the blood work, along with the other test results, over to the specialist at the University of Minnesota for a second opinion. I called to schedule an appointment to see this new specialist as soon as possible, which took more than a casual effort since the guy was in semi-retirement and was finishing research for his third or fourth book to be published by Oxford Press in London. In addition, he was battling a permanent health issue of his own. We finally got the appointment several weeks out.

On the drive home, if my wife and I talked or tried to comfort one another, I don't recall. All I remember is staring straight ahead at the road, looking at

Connor in the rear-view mirror all calm and serene, wishing someone would take care of me and give *me* that kind of peace, because I felt like collapsing. My heart was broken. I had nothing more to give and didn't think I could hold up under the sorrow of not knowing how to handle all this news, uncertainty, and sadness. The trauma around hearing that Connor's situation was LIFE LONG! *What was I supposed to learn from this? And why me? Why me, and my family? Why my first-born son?* This was too much to bear.

I could feel my relationship with my wife moving further and further apart— sliding deeper into our own little cocoons to digest and process what was happening, and hunker down. The stress of caring for Connor, figuring out what we were supposed to do next, and the uncertainty that lie ahead was enough for me to consider throwing in the towel and giving up on life. This was just plain raw, hard, and endless. There was no peace in sight for the Boylan family—none, just more stress and uncertainty. The news had come, and though we'd yet to get confirmation from the second specialist at the university, I was certain he'd confirm the findings. In my mind, we already knew the answer, and it was *permanent.*

I was a God-fearing, former altar boy, and a church-going, high-integrity, hard-working and trustworthy family man. What more was I supposed to do to prove to the man upstairs that I didn't deserve this? I mean, at the end of the day, as all my business friends loved to say, "What the hell? Wow, man…you've got some serious stuff to deal with. I am sorry to hear the news. No offense, but I wouldn't want to change places with you, man. Not in a million years. I don't know how you do it."

Not exactly marvelous words of comfort, though they were probably doing their best despite their confusion about what to say. This was part of the problem, in a sense, because the news was so intense. No one knew *what* to say. What was there to say? When you learn of news that is overwhelming, that comes suddenly out of nowhere, what *can* you say? Some people retract and say nothing out of fear they'll say something dumb or out of sorts. However, we probably couldn't hear anyone else anyway. We were in a state of numbness. At least I will speak for myself, as it's never safe to assume you know or understand how another person is interpreting the same traumatic situation, even your spouse.

I don't know how most people handle traumatic news because I'm not a therapist or psychologist. And who knows if we went through the *typical phases* of the grieving process, but I could really care less. I was numb, angry, exhausted, sad beyond words, and tired of it all. I had had just about enough, thank you very much! It felt as though God was trying to single me out for whatever reason, and I didn't appreciate it—not one bit; not for the life I was trying to put on the boards. I was being picked on in my opinion; harassed; interfered with. That's how it felt. Another *speed bump* in my life, only this one was major league, much more so than my car accident when I broke my back and ended up in a metal brace for years. Connor's diagnosis was *permanent! Forever!* I couldn't fix it or change it. This was hard to digest and comprehend, that I couldn't *fix* or *solve* the situation. I had to learn how to handle it, live with it, change my life accordingly somehow, and find some peace with the whole thing, though that's not where I was at the time. I was angry, pissed off, sad, scared, lonely, and paralyzed. I had busted my butt for way too many years getting my company launched, my first and second books promoted at the national level on CNN, Bloomberg Financial and others, execute a nationwide book tour, train multinational clients on the methodology I'd developed and written about, keep a roof over our heads, pay for the extras like nice family vacations, keep my daughter's private strength and conditioning training going (since she was becoming a very talented basketball player), and all the other things that make up everyday life!

To say I felt as though the wheels where coming off the train would have been putting it mildly. I was tired of the daily grind of it all, and the definitive news about Connor put me over the top. There's only so much a person can handle before they wonder if they're going to break or shut down, and I was there. I was sick and tired of people tilting their heads to one side and saying in their soft little voices, *"You know, the Lord never gives us more than we can handle,"* or *"This is right where you're supposed to be right now."* Well I am sorry, but what the hell does *that* mean? Yes—I'm a God-fearing person, but honestly, how are these comments to be digested when you are sad beyond words, you're at your wits' end, grasping for anyone or anything that can *maybe* help you make sense of it all? I wanted answers from the one above, and felt I deserved them…right now! Was God trying to break me down? It sure seemed like it. In fact, I became convinced I was being broken down to nothing, and He was doing a marvelous job of it. At one time, I thought maybe I was *wired* to the top, being the good Catholic, church-going, family man, with an aunt that's a Carmelite Nun for goodness' sake. Doesn't that qualify for some level of special graces? But this wasn't buying me any points as I kept asking for signs. *At least* I deserved that much, since *He* was giving me a boy with profound special needs.

Being a small-business owner for twenty-some years, I wasn't into this concept of *"find some quiet within yourself"* holistic mumbo jumbo. I wanted a billboard on the highway telling me *why* this was happening, and what I was to learn from it. The pressure was so great I felt entitled to some answers. Why was I *picked* for all this strife and hardship? Was I some guinea pig selected to endure this level of pain, sorrow, and helplessness? And for whose benefit? I kept asking what could be positive in all of this, because based on my assessment, nothing was positive about the situation—nothing at all! I kept praying for answers but nothing was coming, which made me even sadder, scared, and depressed. A stunningly fabulous combination of emotions to have when attempting to grow a business in a difficult economy, putting forth a positive outlook necessary to win business from clients who don't *care* about your personal situation, as sad but true as this really is. In point of fact—remember this: I made the grand *mistake* of sharing in confidence, the news we'd received about Connor a year or so earlier with one particular client who I thought was a heartfelt guy, only to learn after sharing the news that his company was now "concerned" about my level of focus on their account. What a hell of a note! *Guess I can't trust sharing the news with anyone except our closest of friends,* I thought. A friendly world we live in, isn't it? When people *need* some solace, and what you get instead is a totally self-absorbed response that sends a clear message that they couldn't give a rip!

The more I prayed for answers, the more isolated I felt. I became more introverted because it wasn't fair that I wasn't getting any peace. My personality was changing, and this started me down the path of questioning the value of my faith, the core of what I'd been raised to believe since I can remember. Life wasn't fun anymore. And my son had a lifelong diagnosis.

What do you want from me? Haven't I been a faithful servant? I need help understanding why this is happening to me. I don't have the emotional capability to handle a special-needs child, let alone the money for everything he'll need over the course of his life! Why me? This is not funny!

This was part of my prayer life, if you want to call it that, but nothing was coming. No peace, no comfort, and nothing was letting up, just more stress. And Connor *needed* me. He needed to know I was right there, and so did my family. And as cold and unending as everything seemed, giving up was not an option though I thought about it all the time.

Looking back, I can understand that nothing was happening *to me,* though this was exactly how it all felt. In fact, to be honest, it felt like I was being persecuted in some manner, or tested for something to come, though I had no clue as to what that would be, since what I'd been doing for the last several years fit my talents well. And though I didn't have the emotional depth or understanding at the time, the most special of gifts was being given to me, though I didn't comprehend or welcome it. I was just mad, sad, scared, and confused. And I needed help, but didn't know what I needed, or whom to ask. Life was cruel and I certainly wasn't getting any breaks. It was hard to be anything but sarcastic toward the faith I'd be raised to believe in, since it seemed to have all but abandoned me.

There was no love coming, yet I had to muster up a new level of love, patience, and understanding around something I didn't understand. I wasn't a caregiver by nature, but I was going to have to learn by trial and error because this was what my son needed. That's what I would have to become for him. I'd adopt a new temperament and new level of patience. This was going to take a while. I'd need to learn a new calmness, and a new level of trusting in my higher power since everything was well beyond my control. So much so that even attempting to plan my life or anything related to work seemed impossible at the moment—perhaps even stupid, since *everything* was up in the air. To be there for Connor, I'd have to learn to become a different person, to mold myself into a new personality around what this new life was going to look like, as best I could tell. The fear and uncertainty was intense, but I was carving a new charter and a whole new chapter without knowing, basically out of survival.

CHAPTER EIGHT

SHUT THINGS DOWN—TURN OFF ALL THE NOISE

With no sign of comfort, it was time to hunker down and wait to see the second specialist at the University of Minnesota to verify the findings of the Fish blood work test and whether Connor would receive an official diagnosis of Williams Syndrome. Or maybe he'd give us different news —though I doubted it, since these guys were sharp. We needed to be as patient as possible until we saw the other specialist.

I don't recall for certain, but I think we told our daughter, both sides of our families, and the two priests I'd been friends with for years (one of whom married us), the news about Connor sometime after the first of the year. The second specialist would likely confirm everything, so in my mind we already had our answer.

For my wife's and my sanity, we needed to turn off all the noise around us and hope for the best, knowing we were powerless over our situation. Not a great feeling for a guy who likes to be in control of his destiny, especially after having it pounded into my head that if you weren't in control, you would surely end up with a handful of mud, as they say. With everything swirling around us, I stopped answering the phone, reduced parties and outside events we went to (other than our daughter's basketball games), and pretty much kept to ourselves. Winter was here; cold, still, and lonely. Things were frosting up in my mind. I knew I was having trouble keeping everything going, like my attitude and the travel schedule for clients, which sometimes meant going out of the country to deliver sessions. I kept feeling like I needed to be with Connor more and more. There were so many balls in the air, but all of a sudden, Connor needed to come ahead of everything. The volume of medical correspondence back and forth was on the upswing, and it would only increase as we learned more. A new year was upon us, 2001, with lots of doubts, fears, and uncertainty about where life would lead next.

The day we drove to the University to meet with the second specialist, Connor again had such a peace on his face, that it touched me to my core; a piercing calm over his whole person, like some angel from above, no worries and total serenity—as though he *knew* something I didn't. His gentle, soft cheeks made me feel warm as I lifted him into the back seat and got him all situated with Snuffy. My mind was swirling with how everything was going to work for

Connor, our family, our marriage, my job, and me. I've never considered myself a worrier, but I was on the fast track to becoming the world's foremost! And how do you keep fear and sadness from showing on your face? A hard thing to deal with when trying to convince a new client to do business with our firm. Some people are good at faking it when their personal life is in shambles, but that wasn't me. The concern and worry must have shown all over my face, as business slowed nationwide and internationally, thanks to the technology industry meltdown, the dot-com bust, and the market's steady decline. Management and sales training related initiatives where not exactly on the front burner in the executive suites of corporate America. In fact, we were moving into perhaps the worst drought in the sales and management-training industry, which the industry itself didn't see coming. Wonderful timing for me! I was looking for some breaks, but they were not on the horizon. I'd have to continue to grind it out one deal at a time.

As we entered the second specialist's office, I recall a doctor in his 80s who looked like the mad scientist from the movie *Back To The Future*. He had long, silvery-white hair going in all directions, and was friendly and talkative. The whole package made for a guy that was definitely *way* out there. After exchanging niceties, I began.

"Have you looked at the blood work from the Fish Test and other files forwarded from Children's Hospital, like the EEG, EKG, echocardiogram, and other tests?"

"Not really. Don't really need to. I can tell," I recall him saying. He then took over the conversation watching Connor like a laser, as he moved around the doctor's office exploring all the fascinating things.

The doctor began. "When I start talking to Connor in my Daffy Duck voice, I want you to watch what he does with his eyes, and the expression on his face."

Connor reacted just as the doctor had predicted, moving his eyes up and to the left.

"Connor will keep exploring things in my office and eventually find the stereo receiver behind my desk. He'll stop, explore it, and then push the power button on."

Connor did this too! *What was this, some kind of freak show?* I wanted him to look at the test results. That's why we were there—to learn his medical opinion, not watch as he made a bunch of predictions about what Connor would do while in his presence. I wanted the data and his sound medical opinion about whether or not Connor had Williams Syndrome. My patience was running thin. We'd been in one too many doctors' offices, gone through more tests than I could remember, tried more things that some doctors and researchers thought might help that didn't, and now this guy was talking like Daffy Duck and asking us to watch what Connor did next? This was serious! This was my son, and I didn't feel he was taking our meeting seriously. I had been told that this guy was "out there" but also, whip-smart and highly regarded in medical circles around the world for his research and intuitive knowledge of children with syndromes of the head and neck. He was a specialist of world-renowned stature! But he could at least look at the blood work!

"Doctor, have you looked at the medical reports regarding all the tests we've done with Connor? What is your assessment? Do you think he has Williams?"

The doctor became more conversant as he shared that he had actually reviewed the medical test reports and the blood work, and did feel the findings supported the diagnosis that Connor had Williams Syndrome. When we heard his assessment, we began to barrage him with a litany of questions about what to do next.

Since I was resigned to this outcome, expecting him to agree with the blood work and the other doctors, it wasn't as much of a shock this time, though I don't know what my wife was expecting; maybe the same thing. We sat there humbly as he explained in high-level medical jargon, the *gene deletion* that is the essence of Williams, the typical symptoms on the spectrum itself, and all they didn't know, (since being discovered in 1997, as I recall him saying, thanks in part to this blood test called the *Fish Test)*. We listened while trying to comprehend what he was saying, since he was a researcher who was challenged to articulate things in layperson's terms.

So, we had met with the world-renowned specialist at the University and had our second conclusive opinion validating what the others where telling us: our son had Williams Syndrome. He gave us the spectrum of *"here's the good news, the bad news, and the news we just don't know"* about Williams, which left me feeling we were in uncharted territory. This was especially true because the medical community didn't have answers to all of our questions, being a relatively new "discovery." But that didn't stop us from asking questions until we didn't have any more. And when it felt as though there was nothing more he could tell us, other than **we were in for a life of unknowns and major challenges**, he complimented us for being committed parents, extended his office as a resource, and coached us to find a good set of doctors that could help us quarterback Connor's care throughout his life. We thanked him as he explained he was battling a terminal diagnosis himself, and that he might not be around much longer, though we were welcome to call him any time.

I recall thick silence on the ride home. My mind was working so hard it felt like you could hear it winding inside. We had our answer now. A second world-renowned doctor published on children's syndromes confirmed the diagnosis. It was time to turn off all the noise until we could figure out what to do next. I was moving into a state of numbness. Winter, in my mind, might never leave.

I'd been raised to look at the glass as being half full, but wasn't so sure why a positive outlook was beneficial now. It didn't make sense to me anymore. We'd just been given shattering news about our precious son, my first, and maybe, my *only* son. He was our boy, the boy I was going to play hockey, baseball, and tennis with, and watch play high school and maybe college sports. He was the son I was planning to roughhouse with, the son who was going to get married someday and give us grandchildren. All of these uplifting *pictures* housed in my mind for years were now clouded and foggy. I couldn't see them anymore, though they'd been in the forefront of my mind since my wife was pregnant. They were more than likely not going to happen now. And he was just 2 ½ years old.

Ever had your expectations *locked in* because you were *certain* that things would happen *exactly* as you expect, so your anticipation is through the roof? Welcome to all those pictures being stolen from my mind, hopes and dreams about life with my son now dashed. I needed time to digest everything—space to comprehend and figure things out. But there was none of that. My family needed me, and I needed to meet the demands of our clients. The time to let things sink in to comprehend the news would have to come in between everything else, as life kept moving. And I was starting to shut down.

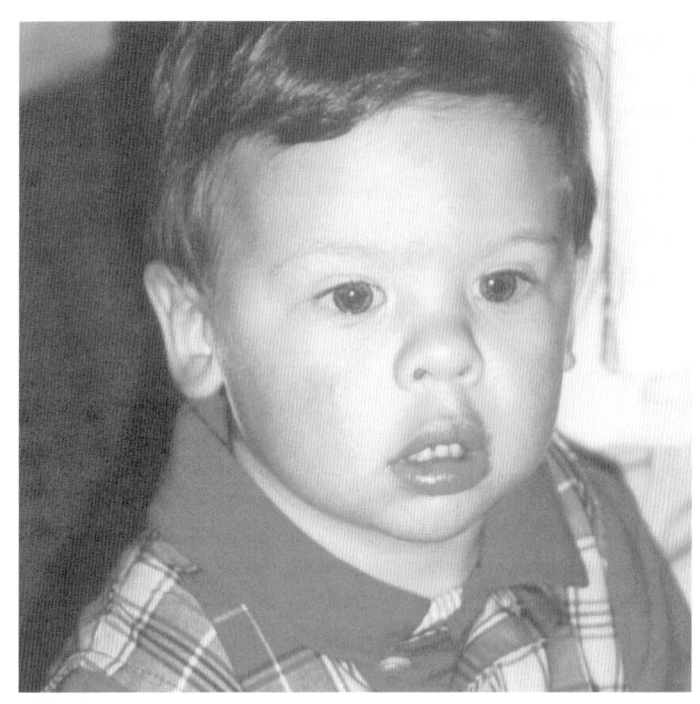

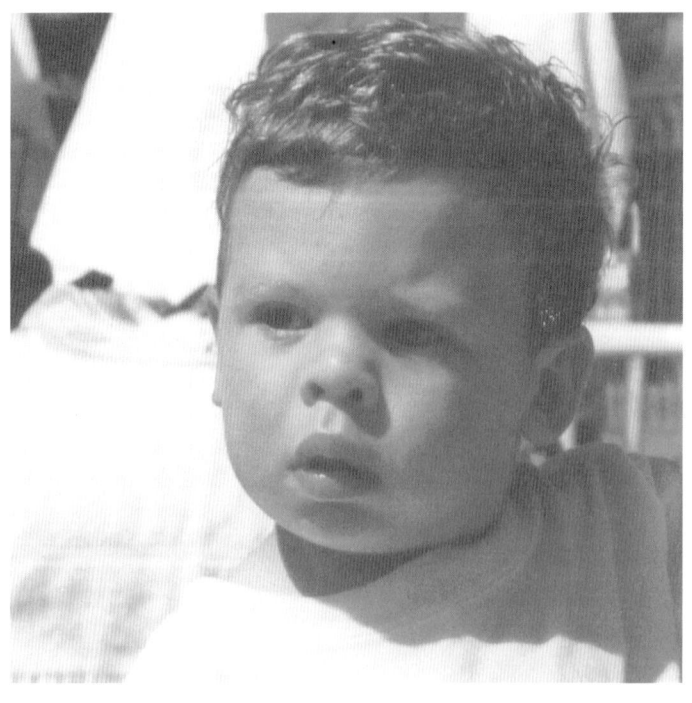

I CAN'T CONTROL THIS! HOW CAN I SUCCEED NOW? —AT WHAT?

Is control a necessary thing to have in order to be successful—control of your mind, your emotions, feelings, actions, and your attitude toward life? And what about control over your work and professional life? Isn't *that* a requirement in order to succeed? It's a grand topic of discussion for men and women alike. I'll come back to this because I don't have the answers to any of the questions, and because it's such a broad area for debate based on whether you're a man or a woman. And your opinions are just that—based on your views and circumstances. There aren't any right or wrong answers, just whatever you believe to be the case. But it's a heavy topic for most people, the issues around control—and control of what? The topic cuts into the very fabric of our beliefs around how we conduct our own lives. It's that deep.

So you can understand why I was having control issues with my *life* at this point, and wrestling with the issue of why it seemed like it was being wrestled away from me by some force I couldn't get my arms around, slow down, stop, or CONTROL! This was adding to my general feelings of helplessness; not a good thing when as a man, society gives you a roadmap that says you're supposed to be *large* and *in charge,* and *on top* of things. At least if you want to be a man, and have the kind of perfect life often portrayed in the media all around us.

I didn't feel in control in any form or fashion, and was beating myself up because of it. I wanted to give up and surrender the fight. I was tired of feeling like my mind was in a vice grip on some workbench, cranked as tight as it could possibly go. But I was still trying to secure that sense of calm, though the harder I tried, the more out of control things seemed to get. I now understand why so many people who are special-needs caregivers, and people going through major trauma in their lives, are in a state of high anxiety much of the time. It makes sense based on the level of constant stress, as there isn't any *end* to it all, when you are the parent or related caregiver of a special-needs child. The care giving *never* ends.

But it's time to be even more honest and say that though I was focused on Connor's needs, I was worried about my family and what this would mean for our life! It's true in many cases that we as a people are quite selfish, even when life-altering news comes out of nowhere. And I would say I am no different. This is why we need help; others around us who can relate to the stresses, fears, and anxieties that run deep, and the emotional rollercoaster of it all. Even when the news is about someone else, such as our son or daughter, we often *first* focus on ourselves and what *we don't have; won't get* or *won't become* as a result of whatever the news is.

Truth be told, this was a big part of what I was buzzing about in my mind. Just trying to deal with how things would work out, not understanding that I could have been more *trusting* that things were going to be okay. But control-oriented folks such as myself want *answers* and we want them now! I had little time for patience since my world was crashing down around me. I felt entitled to answers or at least some level of peace. And since no answers were coming I thought the best thing to do was to grab control of the situation, which in hindsight I couldn't have controlled anyway.

Maybe it's a male thing, but not having control of the situation added to my insecurities of how screwed up and upside down everything had become for us. And that translated, based on my upbringing and mindset, to an unsuccessful person with an unsuccessful life—more depressing still.

My mind wouldn't rest with the potential scenarios about life, work, our family, money, medical insurance, Connor's overall health needs, our daughter's needs as a budding athlete, etc. And my lack of being able to control any of it was driving me deeper into despair and depression, something foreign to me. Being forward-looking for the sake of being positive felt ridiculous to me now. I was done faking it. I was in a fight for my son's care and nurturing, our family's well being, and the *pictures* ground into my mind subconsciously about what I wanted to do with my life since I was a boy. All of a sudden, nothing was on track, in fact, everything was derailing faster than I could blink.

These *pictures* of the way life was going to be with our newborn son were also going to have to be dealt with somehow as *everything* was now on the table: our future, my family's well being, and my own mental and emotional stability. My wife, from what I could tell at the time, though I didn't know the signs of depression or high anxiety in her or myself, seemed to be a trouper, dealing with things in stride, maybe better than me. I'm not saying she didn't have her days, because she did. We both did. But from what I could tell, she seemed to be handling things okay, at least on the surface. On the inside, I can't really say, even though we were married. It's much harder to know these things, since men and women are so different in the ways we deal with and cope with ongoing life stresses, especially those directly related to your children.

Since we were deeply sad and down at various times throughout the week, (though from my recollection, we never talked much about it because it just seemed to hard), we seemed to *assume* what the other was thinking or feeling without taking the time to verify it. Sure, this was a big mistake. I understand that. But in a time of massive stress and anxiety, how many people do you know that actually take the time to see if they're doing everything *by the book,* while focusing on the other's needs and concerns? Nice to consider the textbook version of how to handle tough times, but that's not what we were doing, at least from my perspective. We were trying to deal with what life had tossed our way as best we could. And it's hard not to feel alone, since life continued to move at the same pace. It seemed everyone else's lives were going along quite nicely without much stress or interruption. And then there was The Boylans. *"Hey, did you hear the news about the Boylans' son Connor? Williams Syndrome! Yah, can you believe it? It's just so sad. It breaks my heart. I think it's maybe something like Downs Syndrome, or like Autism or something like that. I don't exactly know for sure, but it's major. He is like mentally challenged. I feel so sad for them. He's just such a gorgeous little boy."*

As they say, news travels fast, so as people in our circle of friends and beyond began to hear the news, we were answering questions like guests on some television talk show circuit, clearing up a bunch of misinformation as stories wound out of control about what Connor did and didn't have. We didn't *have* the answers to all of their questions, giving me an even deeper feeling of being out of control and not in charge of our family or my life.

I was moving into a slow-motion setting on the *life* remote control as if I was outside myself looking in on everyone who would come into our life, do their best to express their concerns and support, then move back to focusing on their own lives, as anyone would. It's just that explaining Connor's situation over and over, and then trying to respond to the next round of questions, such as, *"What are you guys going to do?"* put my mind into a thick fog.

Everything from my perspective was now in a state of flux, like my career. I would need to find clients closer to home to reduce the travel, though I would have to take clients in any location for a while, until I could close deals closer to home. I would need to stay positive, which I was doing a lousy job of. And I would need to wrestle with those *pictures* and *expectations* of what life was going to be like for us with Connor. They were going to be different pictures now, but I couldn't yet see any of them.

The permanency of the news took months to settle in. From my perspective, my wife and I began to drift further and further apart, internalizing our sadness, fears, and frustrations. The focus on Connor and my daughter came first. Right or wrong, that's how it was, and we were last—not a priority, really. Connor's needs were at times all encompassing, so we both tended to Connor first, then our daughter, and if there was any time left, we seemed to somehow not share it with one another.

In my opinion, my wife was becoming even more control-oriented, while I was moving in the opposite direction. And since our marital relationship had been sliding in the wrong direction even before Connor was born, the stress from the news about Connor only exaggerated the gaps in our marriage and the lack of verbal and physical intimacy that had been going on. From my recollection, I had suggested we see a marriage counselor, priest, or *somebody* about our issues. But it always seemed to end in an argument or some version of silence, in which we wouldn't talk for a while, so we never did anything about it. I guess we were both at fault in one way or another.

I don't know how a woman deals with these types of *vacancies* in her life, but I felt unwanted, unattractive, and in a way, not needed or desired *except* for when it came time to writing a check for something. I *got* that part. In those times, the fake, insincere smiles and plastic hugs came out, a splendid reward. Sometimes I got a peck on the cheek. But other than that, we'd become platonic roommates who might discuss being intimate once in a great while, but only followed through with a handful of times every year if that. I was lonelier in my own bed lying next to my wife, staring at her back, than I was in some hotel on the road while delivering one of our programs. It was a horrible feeling. I was married, yet alone. To be fair, maybe she felt the same way. I really don't know because our communication about *us* was poor and so non-existent, that to assume we had a good read on each other was crazy thinking because we seemed to move on assumptions we had about the other more than anything else. Talking about the real issues, whatever they were, seemed too hard now, especially with all the issues we had to focus on for Connor's sake. So, the health of our marriage was put on the back burner and left there to burn. My resentment toward her increased, and I would guess that hers toward me did as well.

I didn't feel as though I could control anything so I stopped trying. It was the mental equivalent of throwing up your hands in desperation and yelling, "Whatever!"

As the news of Connor's diagnosis sank in, we began engaging various therapists and doctors to chart a course to providing him the services that might help his cognitive, fine and gross motor skills, speech development, nutritional needs, gastrointestinal issues, and other needs, in addition to his regular heart check-ups. Learning where to look to find, then manage, all the professional caregivers, their schedules, opinions, and personalities was a full-time job we both shared.

Connor would be 3 years old in August of 2001. He was the most adorable little boy with the gentlest peace about him when he was in a calm state. I couldn't get enough of staring at his face and holding him as he seemed so content, peaceful, and so at ease with life. I *wanted* the calm, inner peace that he had. Life was swirling wildly, but Connor had this calm about him that was alluring. Was he my angel? Did he know inside his mentally challenged mind that somehow things were going to work out okay? I wanted someone to tell me they would, though I had absolutely zero confidence they would. I had the pessimistic thing down quite well now.

On the work side, it seemed my business, which had doubled in revenues four consecutive years, was poised to double again in 2001. At least I had *one* thing that seemed to be going okay. It appeared we were headed for our fifth consecutive year of doubling our growth. We had proposals and contracts awaiting approvals and signatures with Fortune 1000 companies, due to sign in the coming weeks.

I'd wrestle back control of my work life and channel my stress into building the business, which seemed headed for another growth year moving into 2002. I'd refocus the client mix closer to home, as I wanted to spend more time with Connor and my family.

Then 9/11 hit.

How much can one person take before they say, *"Yah know what, this isn't funny anymore. Is someone trying to tell me something? How much more are you going to give me before I break? Is that what you want? Am I some sort of marked man, or just someone who has the worst luck on the planet? Did I do something to deserve all this?*

Almost overnight, no one returned phone calls. The senior people in the companies I'd been dealing with for months went invisible. Proposals and contracts awaiting approvals, signatures, and re-ups dragged on, eventually grinding to a halt. Clients and prospects that were ready to sign contracts went deep into foxholes. Everyone waited. Long-term clients frosted up and no one seemed able to find a phone, or even their laptop to send an email indicating what they were thinking. Just silence. And these were the largest deals I'd ever had. Nothing I had worked so hard to create and close over the last few years was coming in, other than work from existing clients. People turned harsh, rude, and *everyone* was classic non-committal. One by one, the deals I was counting on slipped quietly away into the night, never to be resurrected.

Since nobody was returning calls or emails, I learned the fate of one deal in the *Wall Street Journal* with a headline something to the effect of *"EDS to close EDS University in move to save 16 million."* Magically, our proposal for an initial engagement (leading to a larger opportunity when the pilot proved successful), wasn't going forward now after 18 months of meetings and effort. I learned this as the new year began.

I learned the fate of another client later that year with a call from our banker.

"Hey, Michael. Say, have you seen the front page of the *Wall Street Journal* this morning? Might want to check that out. Isn't that firm one of your clients? We have the contract in our files, don't we? Do you think you'll get paid from these folks? We should schedule some time to sit down and review your line of credit to see how you're situated, as things seem a bit tenuous out there. What's your schedule like this week or next?"

Interesting timing as Norwest Bank was merging with Wells Fargo, and was centralizing decision-making power, making it almost impossible to get an answer from anyone in the Minneapolis branch. But as banks sometimes do, they elected to call our line of credit, after we were honoring all the terms, forcing me to zero it out in short order. I'll never forget that. In my opinion, the only way to truly have leverage with a bank is when you're into them for a ton, so they *must* work with you. In my case, it was a large line, but not for them, and they wanted their money! So they got their money, forcing me to sell more ownership in my firm to pull in more cash. And all the while, I was attempting to get settled into a new life of having a special-needs child, learning new medical jargon, new treatment therapies, seeing if they'd work for Connor, dealing with the times when they didn't work, managing numerous therapists and their opinions about certain types of therapies, seeing if there was any impact on Connor, coordinating their availability for treatments, etc. It was overwhelming, but we didn't have another choice, which compounded the feeling that my head was eventually going to bust.

I was getting no relief, and I'm guessing neither was my wife—though I am not certain, since our relationship was moving into frozen territory. To my recollection, we didn't share our feelings much about Connor, how we felt about the situation, life, or each other. In my opinion, we didn't communicate much, except on a surface level about our daughter and Connor's needs, schedules, doctor's appointments, upcoming therapies, basketball schedules, etc. Life was not warm, gentle, sensitive, or intimate. It was harsh, cold, and *you're on your own pal.*

Succeed in this type of environment? At what? I was just trying to hold on for dear life, maintain the business we had coming in and keep everything afloat. But it all seemed much harder now, and much less fun. I was being lead around by one situation after another, not knowing where or when the next traumatic situation would hit us. It was taking a toll and I knew it. I was moving deep into myself and away from the quick-witted, high-on-life attitude important to convey to others, since people don't like being with a *heavy!* But that's exactly what I was becoming. A *heavy!* And who wants to be around a heavy? Not too many folks I know.

I couldn't break the sadness and sense of loss that had come over me, even though I knew Connor was getting the utmost in medical care from all the doctors and therapists. I watched my medical insurance premiums climb year after year as they put us into higher and higher *risk categories* due to the increasing number of claims. But on a brighter note, all the doctors and care providers seemed to fall in love with Connor, since he was the most sensitive and caring of children. He was a gentle, soft soul that would let you see right into his heart and genuine curiosity for everything. Everything he focused on made you stop and take a second look, since he was fascinated with the simplest of things.

Because Williams impacts chromosome number seven through the deletion of about 20 to 24 genes (according to researchers at the Williams Syndrome Conventions), Connor's brain is not "wired" in the same fashion as what might be considered a normal child's brain. Hence, I might be putting on his pull-up, washing his hair in the tub, feeding him, brushing his teeth, or trying some brushing therapy on his back, and for Connor, though we may have done it hundreds of times, each time was all brand new to him. The genuine wonder and amazement of the simplest of activities around self-care or any other thing, though we'd done them hundreds of times before, would often cause me to pause and reflect at what he found so fascinating. It was as if he was telling me to slow down, chill out, and smell the roses.

Over the next few months, Connor's fascination with the most basic of things, events, happenings, and people began to cause a change in me. I began attempting to see or find a new joy, a new pleasure in the simplest of things, events, or people. In a sense, he was teaching me a new depth of life, a new dimension of appreciation for the basics, which in some respects, started to make me more relaxed. His ability to look at people's faces and intuitively sense if they were happy, sad, or hurting, was amazing to me. He would stare at people's faces, and then mirror their emotion with either a smile or a sad face or a simple comment, like "Daddy sad." He was amazingly dialed into people's faces and their emotions. His soft, peaceful way made me want to be around him all the time.

I would hunt for business, dealing with all the corporate fluff, pomp, and insecurities that seemed so prevalent all of a sudden, that it started to become tiring to me. But then I'd get the chance to come home, take off my suit, and hold Connor as he rocked back and forth, rapidly opening and clenching his fists over and over again. I loved to feel his calm. There was no worry, no fear, and no unrest in him—just a gentle peace, which I badly wanted to feel. I would often just stare at his face, tracing the sign of the cross on his forehead as I watched in wonder, trying to see what was going through his little mind. There was something so serene about him that impacted my soul. I was running on a treadmill, but challenges at home were calling. I was being pulled in both directions, knowing I had to earn a living, yet just *being* with Connor made me the happiest. It felt as though I was being softened, but for what or why, was not at all clear.

The constant strain of life with a special-needs child continued to weigh on both of us as 2002 came and went. We struggled to find breathing room between multiple therapy sessions, doctor's visits, additional tests, and coping with the everyday pace of life, which seemed to get faster all the time. The news about Connor was still settling in my mind and I wasn't prepared nor equipped to handle it on many different levels; perhaps no one is when you receive traumatic news about your child that is permanent. In one sense, it's like a baseball bat to the head—a blow that takes years to adjust to, with some never fully able to adjust. Focusing on work became hard, and that was foreign to me. It made me scared because I understood the need to muster up the willpower to work.

I'd sold stock for an influx of capital so operating expenses and our monthly needs were covered, while riding out the slowdown in the economy as a result of 9/11 and the technology collapse. Battening down on expenses—business and personal—became my focus in hopes things would turn around, and that 2003 would start to improve again.

The management consulting and sales training business had been imploding. One of the largest firms in the country was on its way to becoming half its size in terms of revenues—a sign that things were *not* good in the industry. This gave me validation that it wasn't just me that was having a hard time, since one of the largest firms in the nation was struggling, angry shareholders and all. But it made me nervous about whether I could make it in the current economic storm. I used the time to write my second book while prospecting for new accounts, delivering on deals I'd closed. Things stabilized so our lifestyle continued as it had been. I covered the losses by refinancing the house thanks to the equity built up over the years.

For everything we'd been through, we were holding on okay. Our daughter was making amazing strides in school with her grades, her friends, and on the basketball court. And Connor was making progress with all of his therapy sessions, inch by inch.

It was our marital relationship that wasn't advancing. In fact, moving in the wrong direction, in my opinion, almost to the point of being dead. But I didn't have the energy or the willingness to dig into marital counseling. It just seemed, right or wrong, that it would be unwise to start addressing whatever was so vacant in our marriage. Even though I was unhappy, and I think she was as well, we had *so* much going on in our lives—all of which were priorities. Our children were so important, and Connor needed the lion's share of the attention. It seemed like it would be best to let it pass and maybe things would improve over time.

I did my best to avoid bringing up the topic of *us*, since we were both tired, wired, and often on edge—at least I was, with all the stress from work and home life. And when I did bring it up, which often moved into uncomfortable arguments, I don't think either of us had the energy. It seemed that avoiding the topic altogether made the most sense for the time being. And so it sat there— our marriage, on hold behind everything else, which felt like it should come first. And bless my daughter, because she never seemed jealous over the enormous amount to time and attention Connor needed from me or my wife, a sign of true maturity and an unselfish attitude.

Though things were going along month to month, the constant stress was having an impact. I couldn't smile. I'd see photos of our family over the past few years where my face was expressionless. I'd look at myself in the photos and think, *Where are you? Where did you go? Are you in there? You look like a zombie.*

I was gone from myself. Nothing was fun anymore. Everything was *one big chore*, a grind from one day to the next. I felt *something* was going on inside, though I couldn't articulate what it was. I was being redirected through brute force or by some power attempting to get my attention by grinding my life to a halt. I couldn't understand what was going on. It felt as though something was pulling on my mind, my heart, and me.

THANK GOD the clients we had felt our training programs were of high value. That kept our heads above water. But the constant grind of looking for new clients in a fussy economic time drew so much energy. I needed to be calm, patient, and present for Connor, but it left me drained. Dealing with the corporate B.S. of being told something different by five different people who didn't care much for each other (though they'd put on a great show about how team-focused and committed they were to their enterprise), was all a big joke to me now. It seemed incredibly fake, especially when I had a needy, beautiful little child to care for, protect, and hold.

Trying to convince large and mid-sized organizations that it might be a good idea to invest in helping their sales organizations become more proficient in a struggling economic period fell on deaf and scared ears. Those who said they were empowered to make decisions were nothing more than empty suits hanging on for dear life as they collected their paychecks. Many senior executives didn't know which end was up so doing nothing seemed to be the right call.

Due to the anxiety about Connor and the energy I had to devote to him, his doctors, and therapists, I was losing passion for the material I'd developed—something I *never* thought would happen. A midlife crisis? Maybe. What I did know was my engine was running out of gas. My tank was getting lower and lower, and nothing was there to fill it up; not work, not my wife, nor our friends. And because none of our friends had special-needs children, it was impossible to expect them to comprehend what we were dealing with on a daily basis. When we'd try and explain what a normal day might be like with Connor, they appeared to think we were complaining, so it wasn't worth the effort to share the *real* stuff. No one was able to relate to the loneliness and the total focus required of having a special-needs child. Not that our friends weren't compassionate or sympathetic people; they were. But they weren't living the *life* of a caregiver of a special-needs child, so I couldn't expect them to understand what it was like. So I pulled back from sharing the day to day. It was too much work and I needed to save my energy.

The one person who did fill my tank was Connor. I couldn't get enough of him and wanted to be close to him all the time. We met with therapists, doctors, and other caregivers to help him progress in all aspects; his eating, his fine and gross motor skills, his cognitive development, his hearing, etc. It seemed rewarding and worthwhile, not to mention important.

My life had become unbelievably strange. I'd deliver a keynote address to a group of 150 to 1,000 or more business people—6,000 people at the Microsoft World Fusion Conventions—about the material I'd developed and receive a standing ovation, only to then feel totally alone and under accomplished. Nothing made me feel good or accomplished *except* when I was with Connor, caring for his needs with all the others helping us on his behalf. How weird was this? Not feeling accomplished after receiving a standing ovation from thousands of other successful businesspeople? What in the world was happening to me? This was not like me. At the end of the day, it felt like it was just Connor, Courtney, and me, since my marriage showed with no sign of thawing.

Succeeding had been engrained in me since I was a child. And though we were living in a nice home on a five-acre lot, with nice clothes, nice cars, and nice vacations, I didn't feel one bit successful. I was engulfed by the fact that I now had a special-needs child to take care of—perhaps until I died. I worried so much that I was certain others could see it on my face. It was impossible to relax, and making sure Connor was getting what he needed, and then my daughter Courtney, was about all I could handle. All of a sudden, I was unsure about the direction in which I was headed. That was a *bad* thing, since I'd always been clear on where I was going. Now I wasn't sure about any of that. It was one day at a time now.

Though our marital relationship felt so surface, we both took our responsibilities as parents seriously. And since everything seemed out of control in one way or another, this gave me the feeling that I could do *something* right. I began to take pride in the fact that I was involved mentally, physically, and emotionally with my wife at many, if not most of, Connor's therapy appointments, understanding what they were doing and why, the doctors visits, appointments and tests. I was also *present* at home when I wasn't on the road, which, at its height, might have been nine to ten nights a month. In comparison to a senior executive with a major corporation, I was traveling much less. I was involved in Connor's morning and evening care routines. I wasn't the kind of father who sat on his duff watching television or reading the paper while his wife took care of everything. I was there, giving Connor a bath, feeding him, taking his pull-up off and getting a fresh one, getting him dressed and undressed for bed, putting him down, etc. We were good caregivers. It's just that Connor got the lion's share of our attention due to his needs. Luckily, our daughter seemed to understand why.

Though I was struggling to close deals in a horrible economy, I kept all the balls in the air, but just barely. Enough so my wife didn't have to work outside the home. But to keep her sanity with outside interests, she did have a part-time job off and on during some of the years of our marriage.

I was getting more satisfaction from caring for Connor than *anything* at work, and felt good about it. Control was sliding from me at work, but there was someone who needed me at home. And since we started this chapter talking about *control* and being in charge of your life's direction, I remember one particular story like it was yesterday.

It was one of the *first* telling times where I felt I might need some help dealing with all the stresses swirling around in my head, though I didn't know what kind of help I needed. I just knew I was coming unwound and going dark.

I think Connor was 6 years old when, on one particular morning, I was scrambling to get him showered, fed, clothed, and bundled up, so I could put him in his car seat and drop him off at this Montessori Morning Care program not far from our house. My wife and I felt this place was great for Connor, because of how focused the woman was with him. I don't recall where my wife was that morning. Maybe she'd already taken off for her part-time job. I was getting Connor fed and ready to go so I could drop him off, and carry on to my appointment in downtown Minneapolis. I was hurrying, something very hard for Connor to do. There is no such thing as needing to hurry, as it doesn't register with him; drying him off, putting on a fresh pull-up, brushing his teeth, washing his face, putting his clothes on ever-so-gently so he wouldn't feel rushed, getting his socks on just exactly so, so they weren't bunched up in the toes (which would cause him to fixate on his feet), feeding him some breakfast, cleaning him off again, then setting him on our bed in the master bedroom. I started to get dressed putting on a light gray, single-breasted, three-button suit, a new white shirt, and thinly striped tie in preparation for my meeting downtown.

The new suit fit great and it felt good to be dressed up. Dressed and ready, I picked up Connor and carried him from the master bedroom into the Jeep, got him strapped into his car seat with Snuffy, grabbed my briefcase, put it in the back of the Jeep, jumped in the front seat and turned on the engine. I looked down to find that Connor had gone to the bathroom in his pull-up, and it had leaked out somehow—all over my brand new suit! I sat there stunned and kind of frozen. My new suit was probably ruined now, and there was no way I would make my meeting. I unhooked Connor from his car seat, and carried him back into the house and started to cry. I couldn't *stop* the tears. They kept coming like a river as I sat down on the hardwood floors of our living room, Indian style, holding Connor who was facing me, as he watched me cry.

I sat there, looking up at our 24-foot ceilings in my brand new, soiled suit, holding Connor, and sobbing. Connor kept touching my forehead as tears came down my face, rubbing my head saying *"Daddy cry. Daddy crying?"* He kept staring ever so peacefully as if he was trying to tell me that everything was going to be okay. We sat there until I stopped crying, but I didn't want to get up. I just wanted to hold Connor. Right then, I *knew* I had to change, or I was going to come unglued. I had to somehow change what I was doing to reduce the stress of everything, or I wouldn't be able to cope any longer. Things had been building up for so long, and I now realized I had no control, wasn't going to be able to get back in control, and that perhaps I didn't *need* to be in control. It was a radical concept. I felt like I had 500 pounds of bricks on my shoulders. Just then, the telephone rang. It was my father calling from Colorado.

"Hey there, Michael. What's up? How's your life going? Tell me what's up."

"Dad," I said, "This is not a good time to talk. I am sitting on the living room floor crying and holding Connor, and he just went to the bathroom all over my new suit, which is probably ruined now. I just can't do this anymore!"

"You can't do what anymore? I don't understand," he said.

"I can't do this anymore. I can't move. I am sad and I can't move. I don't know what to do anymore," I sobbed.

"What do you mean, you can't get up? What does that mean? Get up and get moving forward," he said.

"I just need to stay here with Connor for a minute and figure things out. I just need to think. I'll talk to you later." Then I hung up.

I was paralyzed from years of stress building up with nowhere to go, and it all hit at once. Life was totally upside down. I'd moved from successful author, management consultant, and sales trainer to large and mid-sized corporations who thought our programs rocked—becoming required curriculum within several firms, to learning to be the father of a special-needs child, a child vulnerable and beautiful who needed me so much. I wanted whatever he had; his calm, his lack of worry and fear, and his total sense of serenity. I desperately wanted to feel all of these things as the stresses from over the years swirled in my head like some destructive tornado. We sat there on the hardwood floors of the living room, soiled suit and all, holding each other. And while Connor dried my eyes, I thought *I must figure things out*. Maybe I needed some help doing that.

This story stands out as perhaps the first time I began to acknowledge that I couldn't handle it by myself, that I was crumbling inside—and that I wasn't in control of my future, which was playing havoc on my mind, making me feel weak and unaccomplished. I *was* having trouble getting back on the horse of life; stuck in a thick quicksand.

Connor kept rubbing my arm and forehead as we got up off the floor. I took my off suit, changed him into a fresh pull-up, the second of the morning, cleaned him up and dropped him off a couple hours later at the morning care program. Since I'd rescheduled my meeting to another day, I went back to my home office and stared at my laptop motivated to do nothing but cry. *What's going on? I'm in this massive trance and I can't get out of it.*

My being a man in charge and on-the-go was giving way to a more sensitive, deeper understanding of what it's like to feel like you are coming unglued in your work life as you've known it, while your home life is just as stressful, but also sad and lonely. I'd had enough surprises for one lifetime, thank you very much. However, little was I to know there were *more surprises* ahead—things that would bring me to my knees. Stay with me, and I'll bring you inside these wonderful years.

You couldn't have choreographed a worse concatenation of events in a tighter span; learning of Connor's diagnosis between late fall of 2000 and the winter of 2001; attempting to digest the news and begin learning about Williams, finding and building relationships with doctors, therapists, treatments, and all; the shock of 9/11 and the devastation to people's spirits, beliefs, and finances; the freeze on several industry sectors, scaring people and their families, causing them to go numb; and the overall manner in which the business community reacted. I was right there in the middle of it all with overwhelming fear, paralyzing sadness, and uncertainty.

The services we'd been providing organizations didn't seem needed as companies slashed budgets on any training or management consulting initiative unless it was mission critical to the business. Our programs were not viewed that way, regardless of how compelling my arguments that *this* was the time to invest. Deals got pushed into outer space. Multi-national clients with signed contracts began attempting to cancel, reduce their commitments, or not extend options, halting all spending until the country could come up for air and deal with the aftermath from 9/11.

The stress was intense; explaining to investors why over $1 million in outstanding contracts was not coming in; keeping a new bank line in place, and the family income from going into the toilet. All things beyond my control, though it felt like the man from above was out to get me.

I reduced our family budget to less than we'd been used to, but enough to get through the drought until things started moving again. We were able to stay in our home, have two nice cars, plenty of food, money for our daughter's private basketball training and conditioning, business trips, and vacations. Nothing was going into savings, but we'd make it through this temporary drought.

My wife appeared to understand the logic of why we needed to cut back on things while we and millions of other families rode out the ugly economic shock caused by 9/11, the tech sector tanking, the dot-com bust, and the fall-out from all of these shockwaves. Ask people in the investment-banking arena if they got lots of deals funded in this economic period of about three years, and see what they say. It was tough. But my family was getting everything we needed. Thousands of companies had reportedly filed for bankruptcy, so I was aware of how tenuous things were. We'd figure out a way to make it through, God willing.

And though our marital relationship was cordial, respectful, and focused on the children, there was no warmth, no snuggling, no intimacy—at least very rarely. Right or wrong, we had more important issues to deal with so *let's not push it* was my thinking.

You can fault me all you want, thinking it was just plain dumb not to address the issues, but this appeared the wisest choice at the time. It's easy to be an armchair quarterback, but I was picking my battles, and this one could wait until a better time. I couldn't let divorce be an option—no way, even though it had entered my mind from time to time. I considered it an irresponsible thing to do to my children. No way would I ever do that to my special-needs son. I would continue in an unhappy marriage because it was the most responsible thing to do for the family.

My wife was doing a good job holding down the fort when I traveled for client engagements, so it appeared her focus on the kids was as it should be. But what I couldn't see under the surface was that the same stresses engulfing me were starting to show in her, though she was, in my opinion, much better at disguising her feelings. In fact, so accomplished that, when the additional news hit, *everyone,* including me, was in shock. Just what I needed—more shock!

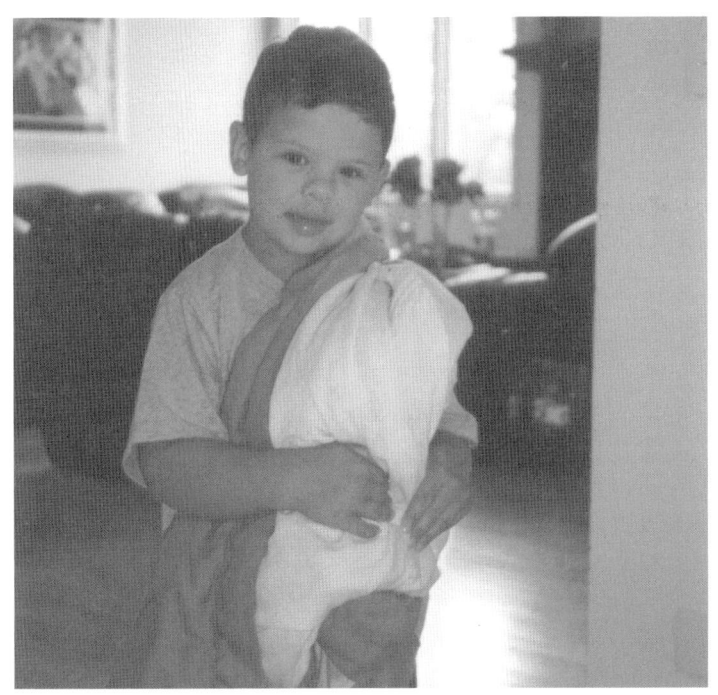

"Snuffy," Connor's purple blanky

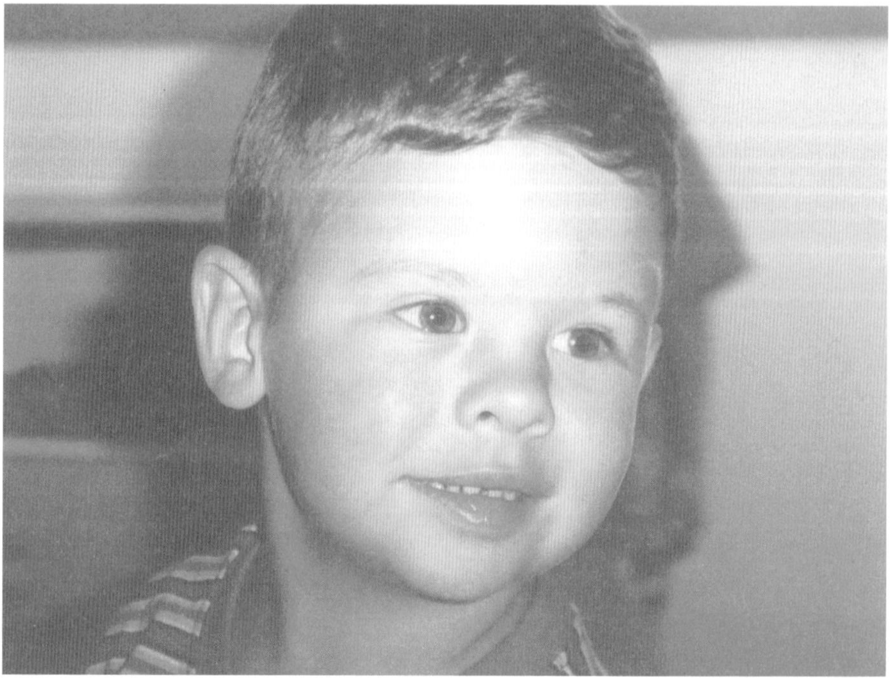

68

CHAPTER TEN

SURPRISE, SURPRISE! THE ICING OF THE CAKES (S)

I was in the office when I picked up the phone to my wife's shaken voice.

"Honey," she said, "I've been in a car accident with the Navigator. We're okay. The kids and I are okay! Can you come right away?"

I flew out of the office, driving north on the main road to find the Navigator on the side of the road, my wife and kids inside, shaken but okay. Thank goodness for a big heavy vehicle. According to my wife, another lady had pulled out in front of her, attempting to make a left turn in the intersection. My wife professed that she had the right of way with a green light. She was *adamant* she had the right of way. The other party didn't see it that way. Our insurance rates went up, the car was repaired, and life went on. The important thing was, no one was hurt.

Several weeks later, in the fall of 2003, while returning from a business trip, my cell phone rang. It was my wife.

"Our house has been broken into. Where are you?" she barked.

"During the day?" I asked. "I just landed. Are you okay? Where are the kids? What happened?"

"I'm okay," she said. "The kids are with me, standing here in the driveway. Police cars are here and the officers are inside checking everything out. Please get home as fast as you can!"

"Stay there in the driveway and I'll be right there," I said.

I flew down highway 494 watching for police the whole way, since I wasn't exactly driving the speed limit. When I arrived, I remember at least two squad cars in our driveway, and my wife shaking as I held her and the kids. I walked into the garage, and in the back entryway to see music CDs thrown all over the living room floor. The stereo components were hanging from the shelves by their cables, yet nothing appeared to be stolen. How weird was that? They were after the sound system but didn't think to bring wire cutters?

The officer was dusting for fingerprints on the sound-system components as another officer approached. He explained that according to my wife, her wedding ring had been stolen along with her watch, some designer purses, some earrings and a tennis bracelet, (if I recall properly). The officer told me to go into the master bedroom closet where I'd find another officer dusting for fingerprints. I followed his directions, to see all my suits on the floor, yet none were missing. The officer was dusting the crystal ring box where we kept our wedding rings, which was chipped. I hadn't known my wife not to wear her wedding ring, since I knew how proud of it she was. But evidently she'd just gotten it back from the jeweler from either a cleaning and/or a repair. And for whatever reason, she wasn't wearing it on this day, and it was now evidently missing, if not stolen.

I walked all over the house inside and out with the officers, and from what I could tell, no artwork, sound-system components, or anything else seemed to be missing, except for her wedding ring, watch, purses, earrings, and a tennis bracelet. We both went down to the police station to be fingerprinted, and I was told they searched the local pawnshops for the ring, but to no avail. I found her watch while searching through the back yard. It was sitting in a pile of grass clippings. She seemed surprised when I presented her with her watch. Her wedding ring never turned up, so insurance paid the claim on the stolen items, and she got a new ring, selecting the same setting I'd given her when I proposed, but a larger center stone. Not the same cut, color, or quality as what I'd given her, but she wanted a larger stone, so that's what she got. Case closed. With all the necessary focusing on Connor, this was another distraction—another speed bump that, as long as no one was hurt, needed to be put behind us. I didn't spend two more minutes thinking about it!

I knew I was going to suffer a loss in the business that year, which I planned to cover by refinancing the house. So, in the fall of 2003, I met with a mortgage banker to inquire about refinancing our home mortgage.

"Yes, Mr. Boylan, plenty of equity in your house. We like to see that. That's a good thing—and a strong valuation on your appraisal, this is also good. However, you have some credit issues, Sir," the mortgage banker said with one eye on me, and the other on his computer screen.

"No, I don't think so," I said, confused as to what he was talking about.

"Yes you do sir," he pressed. "If you are married to a Mrs. Boylan, it appears you have a few more credit cards and accounts with several thousand dollars in outstanding balances," he said, as if to scold me.

"This can't be," I said in disbelief.

"Well, from the looks of your credit report, you have a few more that maybe you didn't know about, all of which would need to be zeroed out if we refinanced your home. Only issue here is that, because of the delinquencies on these accounts, your credit has suffered, so we won't be able to refinance under our standard products. It'll have to be a sub-prime loan, but not an issue as you have plenty of equity. We can still get it done. It'll just cost you a bit more, that's all."

Almost in disbelief, I asked, "How much do these accounts and cards total up to approximately?"

"You know," he said, "Just an approximation here…it looks to be in the neighborhood of between $15,000 and $17,500. Maybe a bit more. Like I said, this is just a guesstimate. So again, as a condition of the refinance, we can zero out these cards and accounts, and get the deal done for you. Sound good?" said with a salesman's smile.

I left not even angry, more in a stupor. Was my wife hiding things from me? Was she lying? What for? Why would she do that? My mind started spinning again. We had a good life, a nice home, nice cars, nice clothes, she had a beautiful black mink coat, we had our health, took family vacations, had plenty of food. Was there something she needed that she wasn't getting? I couldn't image why she'd be lying. All the basics plus lots more were being covered.

I got in the Jeep, started for home, and called her, since she was home with the kids.

"Hi—are there some things I don't know about?"

From my memory of her tone, she seemed to know exactly what I was referring to, and said something to the effect of, "We can talk about it when you get home."

That night, after we put the kids down, we sat Indian style across from one another on the kitchen floor, tears running down our faces. I listened to her explanation of why she had opened the accounts and run up the balances, that she was sorry, and that it would *never* happen again. And that once I zeroed them all out and we cut them up, keeping her on my American Express in the event of an emergency, it would never happen again. We made peace, I accepted her apology, and trusted her word.

We got through Christmas of 2003 and went on a family ski trip to Colorado in the spring with some close friends and their kids, a great and much-needed getaway. We were able to leave Connor with a trusted part-time nanny we'd used over the years, who did a good job with him. It felt good to be in the fresh air of the Rocky Mountains for a week, having the chance to relax without Connor, though I missed him, and I am guessing my wife did too. As guilty as it felt to be away from him for just a week, it was important to have the short break.

When we got back, spring was beginning with my daughter's high-school basketball season now done for the year, and AAU basketball firing up. Busy, busy, busy, go, go, and go. Life was busy, and yet we had this beautiful little boy who needed us to go slower—to be calm, relaxed, and peaceful. It was all *so* challenging to manage. A highly talented, accomplished, beautiful, smart, energetic, athletic daughter. And a calm, mentally challenged little boy who just wanted to be held. Our children were incredibly different, requiring lots of emotional bandwidth from both of us.

As summer approached, we planned a family road trip to Colorado, where my father and his wife lived. While we were there, we'd visit friends over the fourth of July, a great time to be in Aspen. We'd stay in Snowmass where the kids could swim in the pool and we could all just relax.

Call me crazy, but I have pretty good instincts from time to time. The ability to sense if something is not quite right, though I might not know exactly what. Anyway, I sensed my wife was being unusually cold with me, sharp, and very distant. Almost like she couldn't stand me anymore. Hence, the last few days of the trip were tense. Not many words were shared on the drive home across Highway 80 through Nebraska, then Iowa, and up Highway 35W to our home.

A day or so after we got back, my wife and daughter flew off to Atlanta for my daughter's AAU basketball tournament, while I stayed back to work and watch Connor. It was mid-summer 2004 and business was coming back again, thank God.

Question: You trust your spouse, don't you? Well, I did—almost like the back of my hand. So much so that there wasn't any real need in my opinion, to look at the family checkbook. I mean, she was my wife, and she was in charge of it. And if you can't trust your spouse, then whom can you trust? Growing up, I'd observed how my parents, married forty years, seemed to handle things, and from what I remember as a young boy, it was my mom who sat up late at night at the downstairs desk in our living room after we'd all gone to bed, and paid the bills. If it worked for them, then it would be fine for our family. I recall a few years into our marriage, turning over the responsibility of paying the family bills to my wife. This was my wife. We were married. We took an oath on the altar before God, our family, and lots of friends, to be faithful to one another in good times and in bad, 'til death do us part.' I think you've heard those lines a time or two.

So what I'm about to share is hard for me, but you need to understand why I'm sharing it. First, because it's true, and second, it's the culmination—the icing on the cake that brought me to my knees and forced me to look up for some answers. I share it not to bash, defame, ridicule, or dishonor my wife, now my ex-wife. That is *not* my intent, though her actions felt as though she had dishonored me, and our children. I don't want to share all the nitty-gritty because it's too hard, too much, it's like a bad movie, and not necessary. And because the *real* story is about Connor and what I continue to learn from a mentally challenged beautiful little boy.

I guess what's *critically* important in this part of the story, (and why after conferring with others about including it, it was determined that it would help thousands of other caregivers), is to recognize as I've been learning that *receiving devastating, life-altering news* that your son or daughter is a special-needs child, transfers onto the parents and related caregivers a *massive* amount of shock, sadness, fear, anxiety, and uncertainty about how you're going to handle it all—and keep your life halfway moving forward in the throes of caring for your special-needs child.

The important thing to note, at least for me is, where does all that stress go? How does it get released? Where? And in what form? And since every one of us handles massive stress in different ways, you can *never* be totally sure that those under the gun day in and day out are coping just fine! In fact, how would you know for sure? Are you some psychic mind reader? I'm not. I knew I was stressed out, and thought I was dealing with it as best I knew how. And from what I could tell, it seemed as though she was handling everything perhaps better than me! How well do you really *know* your spouse? Now there's a question worthy of days of discussion. My point is; I'd had *enough* surprises over the last five years, with Connor's diagnosis being the biggest surprise of all. I was still getting adjusted. But like I said, there was more icing on the cake yet to come. SURPRISE, SURPRISE!

"Hi honey…um…it is 3:30 my time, 2:30 your time, please call me on my cell. Um…I have to talk to you, it's urgent. I'm going to be coming home; flying home tomorrow morning by myself, um…I have done something terrible, and um, I being very matter-of-fact and cold because, um, I've done something terrible and awful, and um, I need to tell you about it. And um, uh…it's uh…you're gonna hate me, um…you're gonna um, do all sorts of things, you're gonna just freak out. Um…um…there's something wrong with me. Um, and I don't want to frighten you, but I'm just being matter-of-fact because I think this is why over the course of the last three years I've been, um, like I have, um…I can't believe I'm rambling this long on voicemail. Um, call me when you get this please, bye, bye."

I picked up the message on my office voice mail and immediately thought something had happened in Atlanta, so I called but she wasn't answering her phone. I finally reached her early evening.

"What's going on? Are guys all right? What's going on?" I said.

"You know what," she said, "I'm with some of the parents right now that came down for the tournament. But I'm coming home tomorrow morning and I'll talk to you then. What do you have tomorrow afternoon? Gotta go now," and she was off.

Leave me *that* kind of voice mail, and then not tell me what's going on? It was Thursday, July 8, 2004. Another date burned into my mind until I die.

I replayed the voice mail message several times to see if I could figure out what she was talking about, but to no avail. I had no clue, until much later in the evening after I'd fed Connor, given him a bath, done some brushing therapy on his back in the tub, which sometimes worked to help him wind himself down before bedtime, with classical music playing in his room. I put Connor down around 8:30 p.m. An hour or so later, the home phone rang. I answered to the sound of a female voice as she announced through her tears, that she was my wife's part-time employer.

"Is this Michael Boylan?" the jittery voice asked.

"Yes it is," I responded.

"This is your wife's employer." I'd met her and her husband several years earlier at a Christmas party we hosted at the house for some of my wife's co-workers.

From here on, I can't recall the exact words this woman spoke, or in what order, but the key information went about like this:

"Your wife has apparently been embezzling funds from my company and me; it appears for more than two years now, to the tune of over $100,000.00, maybe more, we can't tell yet. Where is she now?"

"She's done what?" I said. "She's in Atlanta at my daughter's AAU basketball tournament, but she said she was coming home in the morning. Is this why?"

"I don't know for sure, but probably," the woman said. "We need to meet tomorrow afternoon and get to the bottom of this. We'll speak tomorrow."

I could have worn a path in the hardwood floors pacing back and forth, as the call went twenty minutes or more. This highly upset woman was crying and carrying on about the violation of trust she felt, asking more questions about my wife, then sobbing. It was awful. I was shocked with the allegations she was making against my WIFE, which were outlandish. I didn't know what to think or do, except to pace back and forth profusely. My mind was in overdrive racing 200 miles an hour. It felt as though my life was one big tragic movie, a new surprise at every turn.

It must have been after 10 p.m. when I called my attorney to share the news I'd just heard. I was buzzing, repeating myself over and over, as he told me to calm down; there was nothing to do until morning when my wife came home. I was up all night, wound like a top!

The next morning she walked into the house and I don't recall if we even spoke; just looks back and forth that to me, told me all I needed to know, that she'd done something horribly wrong. I think one or both of us dropped off Connor at the Montessori morning care home, and then we proceeded to her employer's accountant's office.

I walked into this silent office to find her employer seated quietly behind a desk, her arms folded, and two older men standing at attention next to her as if they were holding up the wall—her accountants, I presumed. I hadn't seen this woman in years yet I reintroduced myself and sat down next to my wife in one of the two empty chairs facing her employer. And then my wife proceeded to explain what she'd been doing in an ice-cold, no tears, cool-headed demeanor and tone, as I recall. She was so cold and collected that I felt as though I was watching a totally different person than the woman I fell in love with and married. This was *not* the same person. This person was cold, calculating, sly beyond belief, and so calm during her explanation about what she'd been doing and how, that it was utterly scary. Was I observing a machine—a person who could turn her emotions on and off as necessary? As she was talking, she handed her employer a white piece of paper that in her own handwriting, detailed a list of the checks she said she had written out to herself over the course of approximately two years, along with the dates of each check, corresponding amounts and check numbers, and a total of what she thought all the checks totaled!

I stared at her out of the corner of my eyes during her explanation, as if it were an out-of-body experience, tissue box in hand to keep my eyes clear thinking, this can't be happening to me! This was unbelievable. And when I heard her say something to the effect of, "Oh, we'll pay it all back. We'll just take a hook on the house," I looked at her in disbelief. I didn't *know* this person. Perhaps, I never really did. She was too cool for my own comfort.

The meeting ended with them saying they were going to hire one of the larger law firms in town with a forensics practice to recreate from the computer files, an accounting of everything they'd alleged was stolen, which might take several months. As we walked out of the office, the senior most accountant pulled me aside and said, "I hope your marriage survives this." I looked up in silence acknowledging his comment, put my head down, and walked out.

I don't remember much after this. Things started happening so fast that everything seemed to run together. We had to deal with Connor, my daughter, her school, basketball, training schedules, attorneys, therapists, teachers, the paraprofessional, medical doctors, my clients, and now this? It was all *so* surreal. This was like something you watched on television! I'd been married to a person who was evidently whip smart, and able to fool people; her employer, her accountants, the bank (which didn't notice the alleged forgeries of her employers signature), me, and God knows how many others. It was unreal that she had carried on like this for what was alleged to be over two years time. I remember my attorney saying something to the effect of, "Do you want to stand beside her in this thing until they determine how much she has allegedly embezzled? Because it clearly sounds as though from what they are saying, it could be north of $150,000."

I said yes.

Upon my return from a short business trip to Denver, I walked in the house to a hand-written note from my wife informing me she'd moved out, taken her clothes, my children's clothes, the Jeep, and other things. The note said not to contact her, that I would see the kids in due time, she was retaining a criminal lawyer to defend her, and that she was also retaining a marital lawyer and was filing for divorce!

I don't swear much—honestly. But on this day I couldn't stop! The person I'd married and was standing by in this whole mess, now wanted a divorce? After I'd just written a sizeable check to her employer on the advise of my attorney, admitting no part in the situation, but that in good faith, I would do what I could to assist her in getting her money back? And now she was filing for divorce? This was the *lowest* of low blows.

I saw my children for the first time on my son's birthday celebration at our house, a half-hour or so before a police car drove up the driveway serving me with divorce papers! This woman was a *machine* with *zero* emotions in my opinion. I'd been hoodwinked. Played like a fiddle, and for what? Or maybe, there was and is some type of mental illness? I have no idea. All I know from my life's path is that those in need of serious help can't be helped until they admit there is a problem, ask for help—then commit to do the work!

After all this came to light, her messages to me were that I was out-of-my-mind crazy for even suggesting she might seek professional help. So, what do I know? I was being trampled, run over by a bus. It felt like I was going down to a place where I didn't believe I could pick myself up again. Like a running back who's fumbled the ball and every time he tries to pick it up, the ball keeps eluding him. I couldn't buy a break and I *couldn't* pick up the ball. I didn't even know where the ball was!

I'm tired of sharing about this horribly difficult period and the pain and sadness it caused my family, friends, and me, so I must stop here. There's more, but it's beyond belief. It kept going for years. Suffice it to say we are divorced and she pled guilty to felony theft in the State of Minnesota's criminal case against her based on her actions. She didn't do any time, even with the severity of the crime, the damage done to her employer, and our family. It's beyond me how someone can violate laws and not receive the type of penalty that might actually prevent them from doing the same thing again. I am not a criminal lawyer, and the one representing her seemed overly cozy with the judges who heard the case.

It doesn't seem right based on the way I was raised. My belief is, had I embezzled that amount of money so methodically over a two-year time span, you'd probably be visiting me in jail. Maybe the judge took sympathy on her because of our special-needs son, and *the new baby boy* she had during this whole escapade with her boyfriend on the East Coast. The Minnesota State Prosecutor could have charged her (based on my understanding) with up to three felony counts based on the amount of funds embezzled. Why they charged her with only one count, I don't know. Maybe it's an overburdened and lazy justice system. I haven't a clue. But the process was hardly impressive. At some points, it seemed like a *grand circus* in which one of the best criminal lawyers in town (by some people's account) seemed to orchestrate the whole show, out-maneuvering and out-lawyering the state prosecutor. It also appeared the judge was too busy, too lazy, or too distracted, to uphold the law. What he allowed surprised many observing the process from afar.

Having gone through the process, I now believe there's a difference in how the law, at least in the state of Minnesota, treats men versus women who commit the same crime. But it's done now! It is over. *All* over. I can truly keep it in the past, thanks to numerous counseling sessions over many years with spiritually based counselors and friends who are Catholic priests. Thank God for time to heal, reflect, look for a deeper understanding, and find the grace to move forward again. And to forgive, which I have done.

My plea for caregivers of special-needs children and all those who are friends and extended family is to be **aware** of the **massive life stresses** and **constant pressures** caregivers are under from time to time—which are almost **impossible** to get away from. And let's be clear—they are forever! It is this constant level of stress and anxiety that can, in some cases, cause people to do things that are not correct or good for them, their families, and society. Therefore, the **critical lesson** here for us all is to be aware, watchful, and helpful to anyone who is a caregiver of a special-needs child. You may be able to help them though a very challenging time, helping them help themselves, their family and special-needs children, and our society.

For the sake of our memories, and because we can all be *unbelievably* quick to point the finger pretty harshly at others about this or that—let's remember again why I chose to share this part of the story. First, because it's true as best I can remember. Second is not to defame, ridicule, or in any other way, discredit my ex-wife. My *primary intent* in sharing is to bring *awareness* to the massive amount of stress, strain, and uncertainty on caregivers of special-needs children, which is real! And to help people recognize that sometimes, this *constant gnawing* can cause people to do hurtful things, causing damage to themselves, their families, and their special-needs children.

This is precisely why we all need to be aware of the constant strain on the estimated 35 million caregivers of special-needs children in the U.S. alone. And why it's smart, necessary, and simply good business, for all taxpayers to make sure caregivers get some help so they can continue to care for their special-needs children.

Was it this level of stress the caused my ex-wife to do these things? No one knows. It can't be used as an excuse to break laws; I understand that. But our family came apart and as a result, *that* is the tragedy here. It has impacted our family and our children, especially Connor—forever!

Was the sadness, constant stress, and anxiety of Connor's needs the impetus for her actions? Was the financial pressure we were dealing with due to the economic slowdown that happened (though the bills and immediate needs were being met), the reason for her actions? Or was, and is it, an illness? These are all fair questions for which I have no answers. I'm not a medical doctor, therapist, or psychologist, so I'm not qualified to say. All I can tell you is how deeply sad and emotionally draining these years were on top of everything else that needed to be tended to in order to keep Connor moving forward as best we could.

The icing on the cake(s) had come and they didn't taste good. The surprises were not happy ones. But as some people say, sometimes, from the darkest hours in your life, (which for me were a continuous period of several years), can come a *genuine* turning point. A true change in your life's compass heading. And though it often felt as though I had no compass heading whatsoever during this period, and that I was treading rudderless in a bottomless ocean of choppy water, this was the event that brought me to my knees and forced me to look up for some help. I needed some peace as all four wheels were flat and I didn't see any gas stations on the side of the road where I could pull over and fill them up. No more surprises! I ask you please. No more surprises. I can't handle any more or I will break!

CHAPTER ELEVEN

WHAT'S THE PICTURE LOOKING FORWARD?

I don't know how you are, but if I can't see the picture forward, I can't function. It's what keeps me going, in a sense. And there was no picture now. Instead, I was on the edge of a cliff looking out over the expanse of water, on the phone with my mother asking for the phone number of my aunt, a Carmelite Nun of 45-plus years. One of the wisest people I know, and the person who called my mother the morning of my car accident, saying something to the effect that my face appeared to her in a dream, that she'd been called to pray for me and wanted to know if I was alright. This was hours before my mom got the call from the hospital in Billings, Montana that I'd been in a serious car accident and had broken my back pretty badly. Ever since then, I felt my aunt was *wired* directly to The Man Upstairs, and I wanted to talk to her. I had had it! I was *so* tired of it all! *What was happening to me, and my life?*

I had no idea what the future looked like for me. It felt like I was in a knock down, drag-out battle with God over exactly who had control over my life! I was out of steam, flat on my back with hardly the energy to look for the positive, since it felt as though I'd been dealt the harshest deck of cards on the poker table of life. There were constant therapist meetings, doctors appointments, clinical evaluations and assessments, heart check-ups, instructional educational plans (IEP is the lingo for caregivers), helping coordinate the team of teachers, therapists, the paraprofessional, and the outside therapists not connected to the school district but through my private insurance, so that we were all on the same page in terms of working toward a common set of goals for Connor.

The IEP was the guidepost we were all attempting to follow to help Connor make progress. My ex-wife and I would meet with five to eight people every six months to assess progress, discuss areas of concern, and make refinements to the IEP as new behaviors emerged. And all handled as if nothing had ever happened between my ex-wife and me—civil and diplomatic. Tell me *that* didn't require some energy! It was all for Connor's growth and development. On top of all this, I had to work! That's right. I still needed an income to pay the bills and child support. (Yes, I had to pay child support, though Connor was with me about 50 percent of the time and my daughter, unfortunately, wasn't living in the house anymore, but with her mother.) I didn't understand how single fathers involved with their children's schooling, teachers meetings, activities and all, kept up the pace. This continues to be a commitment on top of all the care, therapy sessions, corresponding reports, and paperwork associated with getting Connor what he needs. It's not an option to do it any other way.

Because of my personality, I always needed to see the picture looking forward to see where I was headed. The picture of myself had radically changed from Joe Business Boy to full-time caregiver of a special-needs child. It was such a radical change in my self-picture that *everything* was up for grabs now. The image I had of myself had blown up. I felt like an unattractive, unwanted, under-accomplished entrepreneur of 20-plus years, struggling author, management consultant and sales trainer on thin ice, needing to remold my work around Connor, while providing everything he needed. Personally, I didn't think I could do it. I needed to redesign myself into a more calm, relaxed, peaceful, and present father of huge emotional bandwidth for a son so very sensitive, gentle, and tender, so I could be available to him instantly whenever he needed.

It would take time to build this new personality and new person. Especially because of how I was raised; the first-born son of a major-league taskmaster for whom accomplishing the task at hand then moving on to the next one was key! It's what life was all about—getting things done! But it seemed that now, *that* wasn't important anymore. Instead, it was about being *present* for Connor in every way. It sounds so simple and basic, yet very hard to do.

Becoming a calmer, more relaxed, less paced person is what Connor needed. But in reality, it was also what I needed or I'd blow up! The old me would need to go away now—be put in a box and laid to rest. A new me would need to be born, tailored to what he needed: a gentler, slower-paced, relaxed life. How I'd go about this transformation I had no idea, but I knew it was paramount, or we'd both go in the tank! I had no other option. I'd have to change my work life somehow. I'd have to manage therapists, paraprofessionals, and other caregivers, most of which were women, in our case. I'd have to create a super-organized system to keep up with the volume of correspondence and paperwork, which was becoming intense. There was and is often daily correspondence between his teachers, the paraprofessional, and therapists, since without a full-time paraprofessional Connor could easily disrupt the flow for the other 20 or so children in the classroom. The picture was definitely going to have to change to satisfy Connor's growth process in all areas.

The hardest thing for me in all of this was feeling as though I was in a constant wrestling match with God, and that at every turn, I was being pinned down on the wrestling mat of life. Forced to listen, and ask for guidance. The feeling was this strong! I kept asking for some PEACE—GOD DAMN IT! That would be nice! How about just a smidgeon of peace and calm?

Each day, I put on soft music around 7 a.m., the time Connor typically started to wake up, regardless if he was in my bed, or his own bed across the hall. Yanni, Enya, soft piano music, Andrea Bocelli—any music that helped him wake up to a gentle environment, which helped throughout his day. This became part of our daily routine when he was with me, as the schedule became one week with me then one week with his mother, and so on. It's been this way for a long time now—years.

Everything was and still is about *structure* and *routine* for Connor. Creating schedules showing him pictures of the five to six activities in a row we'd need to complete as part of our morning routine seemed to help his mind process what came next. We stuck to a routine when he was with me. I'd make his lunch before he got up, write in his daily diary that went back and forth between the paraprofessional, his mother and me so we could keep in close communication about how each day went; take off his soaked pull-up, put on a fresh one, brush his teeth, let him relax and chat with Snuffy his blanket, talk to *the bug* (another imaginary friend) and play piano in the living room. Then we'd go downstairs so Connor could *pound* on the drums (which helped his entire system to fire), then breakfast, shower, hair dried, lotion on, get dressed, and off to school at 9:15. I'd visit with the paraprofessional about how the morning went, which would definitely impact how his day went at school. Connor had therapy after school two days a week, which was in addition to the therapy services he received during school from additional professionals. It all became routine fast because it had to. Connor *had* to have routine. His brain *had* to have it. Any other way caused too much strife for him.

I'd restructured things so my new window to work was essentially 9:45 a.m. to 3:30 p.m., during the weeks I had Connor. I'd pick him up from school at 3:45 p.m. then we'd go to therapy from 4 to 5 p.m. two days a week. When there wasn't soccer, we'd go straight home to play, and then have dinner. I'd read to him, and snuggle in front of the fireplace with blanky, which helped him wind down before bedtime, around 8:30 p.m. If I wasn't wiped out by the time he went down, I'd work until I was too tired.

This became my new life, totally focused around him. I never thought I'd need to become a full-time mom and a dad, but that's exactly what was happening. I became a 360-degree parent of a beautiful and mentally challenged first-born son.

One particular morning, Connor had a cold, so I let him sleep until after 8 a.m., causing a bit of a rush in our morning routine. He awoke to calm music, chatted with Snuffy, I got him fed, brushed his teeth, wiping his mouth thoroughly so no toothpaste residue was on his face (which caused him to fixate on whatever it was that was still on his face), then led him into the shower. I held his hand firmly, since his overall balance isn't the best. (It has something to do with his vestibular system, whereby if he's not totally centered, he might just wipe out. He sometimes operates by bumping into things, then re-tacking after he hits something; a wall, a pole, people he sees in front of him, but walks right into them, etc.)

Anyway, we were in a bit of a rush on this particular day—my fault for not adjusting to him. I got him into the shower with me, turned around for just *two seconds* to grab the shampoo to wash his hair, and WHAM! He wiped out, hitting his head on the glass wall of the shower. So there I was—holding my child on the floor of the shower at 8:45 in the morning, while most people have already been at work for an hour, water pouring down on both of us, as my son sobbed, and sobbed, and sobbed, me rubbing his forehead as I held him, trying to calm him down.

All I could think was—THIS IS MY LIFE NOW! This has *got* to be a test—*and a test I will not fail! It's just such a radical shift,* I kept thinking.

I used to get up around 5 a.m., work out, and get to the office by 7:30 a.m. to begin the day. Now I'm giving my son a shower at 8:45 a.m. as he cries and cries, repeating over and over again, *"I bonked it,"* as he points to his head.

It was as if I was outside myself looking down on Connor and me on the floor of the shower thinking, *"Okay, it's going to be okay. It's g-o-i-n-g to be okay. Just calm down...c-a-l-m down."*

As I lifted Connor from the floor of the shower and grabbed a towel to dry his eyes, he looked up at me, smiled, pressed his face right up against mine and said in the happiest voice, "I know you! You're a nice boy! Aw Daddy. You're a nice boy!"

Wow! Just another one of the many *immediate* shifts in moods throughout the day, this one delightful, almost like an angelic reminder of how special this child is to me. I never knew when the swings were coming, but it didn't matter, since they are so frequent. It was part of the foundation for becoming a calmer person, so I could more easily handle the swings and be present versus all stressed out when they came on.

The picture looking forward was way too fuzzy, almost like there was some kind of writer's strike, and the scripts for the coming series hadn't been written yet.

HAVE SOME FAITH, MAN! YOU'RE NEVER GIVEN MORE THAN YOU CAN HANDLE

Whoever said this has *never* lived through massively difficult times! At least, that's what I thought. I'd *never* had the wind taken out of my sails like this before. I thought eventually the winds of my own internal motivation would pick up as they always had before, and I'd be sailing along again in no time. That had always been the case before with other challenges I'd encountered in sports, life, and business. But that didn't happen this time. In fact, I went in the opposite direction on some *path* for a deeper set of answers, as I constantly threw out questions about what this was all about—and why? Why was *He* after *me?*

"What do you want?" I would scream, where no one could hear me. If I asked ten times, I asked it a hundred times a week. So much had happened in rapid succession that it truly felt as though someone was trying to speak to me, deliberately slow me down and get my attention by grinding me to a halt. I didn't know if my internal winds would ever pick up again. I'd been halted for some reason, and I started looking *up* for the first time in my life for answers, but through a deep anger and resentment because I was sure I was being singled out, picked on, and given undue levels of stress I had no capability of handling.

It felt defeating that everyone around me seemed to be sailing along with a strong wind at his or her back. A gentle glide path up and forward, with life being relatively free of obstacles. But not for me. Every time I attempted to get back on the horse in the business I'd been in for 10-plus years, bigger speed bumps appeared. It literally felt as though someone was sending a message that something different was ahead. But still no pictures of what *that* was. It was maddening. I had to make a living, and the stress of reshaping my business around Connor and the care he needed was, and still is, challenging. Was I being buffed for something else? It would be nice if I had a clue about what *that* might be. I wanted to be left alone so I could get back on the horse, and ride into a successful life. Problem was, my whole picture of success was in flux.

"Are you okay? Is everything all right? You just seem so different now. You're so quiet these days. Don't you want to join us for dinner?"

This was a typical comment from friends during this dark and lonely period of adjusting to my new personality. I preferred to be alone with Connor. And during the off weeks when he wasn't with me, I kept to myself. I missed both my children, and having an empty house was depressing. Perhaps I was becoming an introvert. Who knows? I just wanted some peace, some grace. I was searching for answers. The concept of faith made sense, but I'd been beaten down so thoroughly, I didn't see the benefit anymore. Faith? For what? It certainly hadn't played out very well for me so far.

Have some faith, Man? I needed to find some—and fast. Was anyone going to turn on the lights in the near future so I could find my bearings, and figure out how to move forward again? That would sure be nice.

Who doesn't like control? Kind of a dumb question since we all know that having a handle on the direction you're headed is a good thing, and a necessity of sorts. Problem is, you need to be driving the bus to control its destiny, and I wasn't driving anymore. I'd been tossed out of the driver's seat and told to sit in the back for a while. To be more honest, I'd given up wrestling for control of the wheel since I was at my wits end and was convinced *someone* didn't want me driving; instead, to chill for a while and be patient! How nice! *Be patient for what?* I kept asking.

If you're not in the driver's seat of life, we all know you will surely end up in one of a hundred places; exactly what I was worried about. Like we talked, control wasn't mine. Leverage? Determination? Internal motivation? They'd all passed me by though I hadn't signed up for any of it. I *was* a driver, but the wheel had been given to someone else now. The old tapes in my mind since I was a boy—about making sure I was firmly in charge of my family's destiny––were all being challenged to their core now.

Self-doubt is a killer drug and I'd overdosed on it for the last several years. Worry and fear was all over my face. I couldn't get rid of it.

One spring Thursday, I picked up Connor from his Montessori school at the usual time. On this particular day he came at me in a beeline yelling, *"Daddy! Daddy!"* falling into my arms in a full-on collapse. He'd had it *locked* into his mind since morning that when we got home, Joe, the lawnmower man, would be at our house to mow the yard. This was the highest of highpoints for Connor; watching Joe, Carlos, Jason, and Matt—the lawnmower guys, as they mowed, trimmed, and weed-whacked their way around our yard for a good couple of hours. Connor would sit on our front stoop, totally mesmerized, rocking back and forth, as he watched ever so loyally as they made their way around the yard. Hog heaven for Connor! *Nothing* beat this! He was in overdrive when they were at the house. And when they weren't, he talked about Joe ALL THE TIME! Something about Joe, combined with the sounds the mowers and whackers made, was music to Connor's ears, though he'd cover them while they were doing their work, or wear headphones to lessen the intensity of the noise.

On this beautiful afternoon, we sat together on the front stoop, waiting for Joe and his crew to arrive. Connor asked about *every 180 seconds* if Joe was coming. With every car that passed, Connor would stand and yell, "Joe is coming. I know Joe is coming. Oh, there's Joe. Here he comes!"

I needed to be calm in these times because he was literally beside himself with anticipation, rocking back and forth, fists opening and closing as fast as he could go. Being calm in these times took *lots* of energy and patience.

Around 6 p.m. after being asked 100-plus times if Joe was coming (and responding as if I'd never heard the question—calm and gentle), the phone rang. It was Joe. His mowers had broken down and he wasn't coming today; maybe tomorrow if he could get them fixed. Connor, unable to comprehend or process why he wasn't coming, just that he wasn't, went into an uncontrollable sob—a lonesome cry that overtook him, moving him from high-as-a-kite elation moments earlier, to utter sadness all in a few moments. *Stay calm*, I kept saying to myself. I held him as he sobbed and rocked back and forth. Then, after about ten minutes, he stopped, looked at me and said, "Tomorrow? Joe is coming tomorrow?"

I couldn't answer with a hopeful response because he'd immediately *lock on* and begin the fixations on the next day, which of course would end in disaster if Joe didn't show up. I tried not to mention Joe until I knew he was within earshot. That lessened the angst.

"We'll see honey, we'll see," I said, as I rubbed the tears from his innocent face. I wasn't up for another day of this so I couldn't tell him. Fixations were, and still are, *huge* for Connor and there are many different kinds; trains, mowers and blowers, the car wash, candy, saxophones, loud noises (which can set him off), and many more. And newer fixations appeared constantly, like later that night, after I'd gotten him wound down and was feeding him some dinner.

I tore off some paper toweling, put it under the faucet, put some soap on it, and began wiping off the kitchen counter as I'd done a thousand times before, in front of him. But not this time. He started yelling to stop, kicking the kitchen cabinets with his feet, covering his ears profusely.

"What, Honey? What?" I said trying to understand what was wrong.

"Stop that noise," he barked, as he began crying again. "Hurts my ears."

This sent Connor back into a high-anxiety state, adding to the wind-down time. I'd need to begin that pretty soon, to get him calm and ready for bed.

Later that night, after playing music and reading to him, it was time for bed. We went through our routine: brushing his teeth, then potty, then jammies, prayers, etc. However, oftentimes, Connor's brain doesn't tell him when he needs to go to the bathroom, and sometimes—there's a mad dash to the toilet.

Even after we've gone, twenty or so minutes earlier. It can happen in the car, on the soccer field, in the grocery store, in a gondola in Colorado, anywhere. Sometimes we make it in time, sometimes we don't. I'd just taken him potty thirty minutes earlier, so I thought we were in good shape.

"Hurry, hurry, hurry," he started chanting. I knew what that meant. We spun around to the toilet, quickly helping him pull down his jammies and pull-up, but not in time. Connor let it fly with fire-hose intensity all over my hand! Standing there, with my hand dripping wet with urine running down onto the floor, I thought, *This is hard!*

This was the second time today he had urinated on my hand because we didn't make it in time. (We usually have about 30 seconds after Connor tells me.)

Remain calm, I kept telling myself; *It's not his fault. He can't help it, and he's not doing it on purpose. This is not about you! It's about taking care of him,* so *just chill out.* I kept repeating in my mind.

I never know when things are going to hit, so it's challenging to remain centered and not *on edge*, since this became another normal day for Connor and me.

I got us cleaned up, put another pull-up on him and we were finally ready for bed. Since the divorce, I'd had the toughest time keeping him in his own bed. I don't know why, nor could he tell me, other than he was scared. Separation anxiety? Don't know, but I wasn't going to give him the third degree. If he wanted to sleep in my bed, then fine.

I got him all tucked in with Snuffy, made the sign of the cross on his forehead, said our prayers, climbed in, read him a story and then turned out the light.

Around 2 a.m. Connor awoke and sat straight up like a steel pole, scaring the hell out of me. He started rocking back and forth, covering his ears because he could hear a train (miles from our house) and it hurt his ears.

"Daddy, what color's train? It hurts me. What color is…red?"

"I don't know, Honey, I don't know, Connor. Daddy hold your ears until the train goes night-night, okay?"

Sometimes the train horn, as he called it, would go on and on. I'd hold him as he rocked in tears because the noise hurt so much. More tears again at about 4 a.m. when he heard another one from a dead sleep. Not a good night. I was exhausted. Up at 6:30 a.m., Connor took Snuffy and went into the laundry room, patiently peering out over the washer into our front yard. *"Joe is coming? I know he's here."* I wasn't ready to deal with the Joe issue just yet. Another day had begun and we'd do it all over.

Expectations can be good and bad, sometimes harmful to your mental health. They can cause huge levels of stress, anxiety, and anger when the things *you* want, expect, or have been planning on happening just aren't or never will. I was coming to grips with the fact that this new life was the way it was going to be for as far forward as I dared look. I didn't expect any of this. I was learning to be an ever-calm, sensitive caregiver, relying on vast amounts of emotional patience to help my mentally challenged *Angel Child*—a child that needed me more than I ever expected, perhaps for as long as I am alive. I didn't expect that one! I thought my son would grow up playing sports of all kinds like his dad, have tons of friends, a relatively easy childhood, go to college, get married, and maybe have some children someday. You know, the typical American dream; the *normal* track that it seems so many people follow. But maybe most of these things would never come true now. Should I wallow in self-pity because I'd been cheated out of having a child with a more *normal* upbringing? Or learn to reshape my own expectations into a new set that were being molded day by day? I knew the right answer.

True, I didn't sign up for any of this, but does anyone sign up for his or her life? It just felt the one picked for me was something well beyond my capability to cope with and manage. But there was no choice; so learning to change into a *new person* was the way it was going to have to be. End of story. A 360-degree father (and mother, since I was single and had no help when he was with me) was the bus trip I was on now. I wasn't driving anymore, and needed to get comfortable with that fact, or it would drive me nuts! Control Boy needed to chill and find a new level of peace in being gentle, present, and calm for my son.

How do you get when you've been pushed to the wall by your kids or whomever, and you feel as though your life is no longer your own, but in fact like you *work* for them? And you feel like barking, *"What am I, your servant?"* This is exactly how I felt, wondering if there was anyone else in the country whose life had been upended like mine, and forced to reorganize everything in order to focus on my special-needs child. My work life, business relationships, friendships, personality, you name it—it all had to change in some fashion to accommodate what Connor needed.

Lying in bed one night during a week when Connor was with his mother, I was doing a marvelous job of feeling sorry for myself. My whole life seemed to revolve around Connor—from the time he awoke to the time he went down. There were also follow-up emails to therapists, his paraprofessional and teachers, adjustments to his IEP, frequent assessments of his progress, tweaking of his occupational and physical therapy plans and related sessions, doctors appointments, etc. Oh—and work stuff too! Somewhere in there I had to work.

The night was quiet, a rare moment to myself. I reached over and grabbed *The Purpose Driven Life* by Rick Warren, a recent purchase based on the recommendation of a few friends. Maybe I'd find some comfort from the thing. The book fell onto my stomach opening to the beginning of chapter 25 entitled, "Transformed By Trouble." How weird was that—especially since my life seemed like it had become one massive series of troubles, one leading to the next?

I began reading, yellow highlighter in hand, when I was drawn like a laser beam to the following passage:

> *"God uses problems to draw you closer to himself. The Bible says, The Lord is close to the brokenhearted; he rescues those who are crushed in spirit."*

THAT WAS ME! I was brokenhearted. Is *that* what he was doing? Drawing me closer to him? What for? Things always needed to line up for me. The paragraph went on:

> *"Your most profound and intimate experiences of worship will likely be in your darkest days—when your heart is broken, when you feel abandoned, when you're out of options, when the pain is great—and you turn*

to God alone. It is during suffering that we learn to pray our most authentic, heartfelt, honest-to-God prayers. Problems force us to look to God and depend on him instead of ourselves. You'll never know that God is all you need until God is all you've got!"

This phrase hit me like a lightning bolt. I read on as if He was speaking directly to me. Maybe He was.

"There's a Grand Designer behind everything. Your life is not a result of random chance, fate, or luck. There is a master plan. God is pulling the strings. God's plan for your life involves all that happens to you—including your mistakes, your sins, and your hurts. Under pressure, your faith-life is forced into the open and shows its true colors."

I lay there rereading these phrases, soaking them in. It *did* feel like He was speaking directly to me, and it felt warm and safe. *Was this all part of some grand design? If so, what for, and what's the design?* I asked. I'd LOVE to know. Then I read one more phrase:

"If a jeweler's hammer isn't strong enough to chip off our rough edges, God will use a sledgehammer. If we're really stubborn (me in spades) *he uses a **jackhammer**. He will use whatever it takes."*

This phrase stopped me cold. This was happening to me! He was using a jackhammer on me to get my attention! Holy buckets! This is real. So why does He want my attention? For what? Was Connor being born to me, and were all the crazy and horrible things that had happened all part of the Grand Design to push me over the edge? Why? What did He *want* from me, or what did He want me doing, for that matter? Actually, I just wanted to be left alone, since it felt as though I was being badgered, picked on, pushed to the limit, and singled out. It was amazingly weird. It felt like I was being hunted and couldn't get away. And trust me—I was trying. Trying to bring my own *plan of attack* back from the dead, but every time I did, new obstacles were thrown in my path. What in the world was happening? What's the big secret? I'd really love to know, damn it!

These questions came out in machine-gun fashion, though the answers didn't come overnight. They unfolded over the coming years as various signs came through unusually coincidental events; the timing of them and their significance began to create a road map to a place I couldn't quite see yet. But clearly, a path was being carved out with me trying to make heads or tails out of which way to follow.

I did feel I was being whittled down to nothing. My confidence was in
the toilet, not a very attractive quality. My self-esteem was non-existent. My
former upbeat outlook on life was nowhere to be found. Why? What a total
waste. This *can't be* what I was called to do—be a sourpuss.

I kept on reading about surrender and surrendering; surrendering unto HIM
and asking for direction and guidance. I thought I'd been doing that, but evidently, not enough! **And if you think this all made total sense to me—you are
nuts!** It was so confusing; since this was the total *opposite* of everything I'd
been taught about how to get ahead in life! I was taught that those who took the
bull by the horns and pressed forward, *those* were the people who got ahead in
life. Those were the folks who made things happen—*made* something of themselves and succeeded in life. You didn't accomplish great things by surrendering! Impossible! I mean, for crying out loud, no way could you get anything of
significance done by surrendering; by being a wall-flower—meek, congenial,
and blowing in the wind. Who succeeds with this type of bent on life? Show me
one person and maybe I'd consider taking on a new angle around this thing
called *surrender*. No way can you accomplish anything by surrendering!
Though there was this one guy named Jesus who actually did accomplish quite
a bit in the world through surrender.

After months of pondering the concept of surrender and what it meant to
me, the weirdest things started happening. I started to gain perspective, become
calmer and not so wound like a top. A level of peace came into me that I'd
never experienced before. The surrender concept started to find a home in me
as I began to ask for more direction and peace, more frequently than I'd ever
done before. It felt good actually, and still does. It seemed to help prevent me
from getting wound up about this or that. It's not magical, but it helped keep me
from fixating on how things were all going to come together. Was this some
transformation I was going through? I can't say, because I don't really know.
But I was learning to serve Connor and all of his needs, and as life went on, I
gained more serenity from surrendering from life as I once knew it—fast-paced
with all the goings-on, traveling throughout the country, meeting influential
people—to a simple existence around my new life of caregiver to my son.

True, I didn't have a choice. But my former lifestyle could have sent me to
my grave sooner than later if I didn't learn a new pattern of life around my son.
Forced to learn it? Sure, you could say that. But I started to feel that through surrender, I would learn a new depth and meaning to life that I'd never experienced before.

"What am I, your servant?" In one sense, I was learning the answer was yes, and feeling empowered by it. Maybe even lucky that I'd been given a mentally challenged son who was teaching me more about life than any teacher I'd ever had. Was I lucky to have a special-needs child with all that that meant over a lifetime? Yes, was my answer, and I found that answer through surrender.

WHAT WILL I LEARN AND WHAT AM I SUPPOSED TO DO WITH IT?

Here's another fabulously creative approach to allowing control to enter right back into my life, after I was doing a pretty cool job with this new concept of surrender.

As clients, associates, and colleagues began learning I had a special-needs child, some would say things like, "Wow, that's got to be tough, I mean really tough. I just can't imagine. But at the end of the day, what have you *learned* from it?"

It's funny how we're all programmed in one way or another, around **business** and the need to quantify how each *situation* is to be learned, extracted from, and then applied. As if we're all trying to climb that ever-invisible ladder to the sky with a better job, better houses and cars, fancier clothes and trips, bigger lives, and much cooler friends, as we rise above the fray to hang with the big hitters. It's like some academic exercise designed to help quantify *the experience* so that it can then help us get to that next level. It's also sad to learn how wired we are to the concept of climbing to "that next level." God forbid we go backwards in life, like I'd been doing—in my opinion—for the past several years. I had nothing to show for it in terms of economic gain—usually how most of us measure whether we're moving forward or not.

But I *did* start asking myself these very same questions. What was I going to do with this new, gentler personality I was taking on? And what was I going to do with the new skill sets I was learning around how to care for Connor, in a world where the woman traditionally has been more of the nurturer, the care-giver, the one who was always there? I don't know if the stereotype has much relevance anymore in our times, but I was sure learning a lot—some of it painful and massively time-intensive. But maybe it would end up being of value to someone someday.

One thing I *have* learned since taking on more of an introvert's personality so I can be patient and calm for Connor—and more observant—is how incredibly self-consumed and self-impressed many of us are from one day to the next. And how harsh we are about *other people's* life interruptions—as if they did something to *deserve* their misfortune and *lifelong* stresses. And how most of us are exceptionally talented at inventing impressive-sounding rationales as to why it's not really our "gig" to understand the strains on parents and related caregivers of special-needs children—the **35 million** or so **caregivers** just in the United States—because, as many people so eloquently put it, *"This might sound really bad, or cold and callus and harsh, but at the end of the day, I'm sorry, but I don't see how this whole thing, as horrible as it is for some people, and I wouldn't want to change places with them for all the tea in China—but I don't see how it impacts me per se. I'm just saying. Do you know what I mean?"*

To that attitude, I say what a **cop-out** and a **total shame**, because this issue *does* impact **every single corporation**—and the state and federal government (meaning all of us, unless you're not a taxpayer), to the tune of **billions** and **billions** of dollars each and every year!

However, I'm a big boy who understands that it often takes a major life jolt or trauma to cause most of us to wake up, pay attention, and look at things outside of ourselves, and through a different lens. And though it's hard to admit but very true, it usually needs to impact people in their pocketbooks in a significant fashion, and then magically, you've got their attention! As the political pollsters like to say, *"It's the economy stupid!"*

As my life has been jolted, I have certainly taken on a different *lens* as a caregiver of a special-needs child. This new lens has caused me to take notice of this incredible harshness within many of our personalities, right there under the surface. We may make comments about other people's misfortunes, without even thinking about who's listening, or how others could be devastated or depressed, as they try to make it through another day as a caregiver of a special-needs child. Here is what I mean.

I was beside-myself excited when, after being fairly persistent with the local soccer organization, I was able to get Connor signed up on a spring recreational soccer team. At 8 years old, this was his first experience in a team-oriented sport, though I knew and didn't care that he had not *one ounce* of competitive spirit in his body. To him, winning and losing didn't register. It was not important. Feelings were important. Is there a lesson here?

Connor was so proud to learn he was on a team with other boys who had the same color jersey. This was huge! The practices were trying. I attempted to keep him focused on what the coaches were trying to teach, since his typical attention span on any one thing can be in seconds, not minutes. It depends on what it is. But he was having so much fun being part of a team, a new experience for him.

At the first game, new purple jersey on and beaming from ear to ear, the coach called his name. *"Connor Boylan. You're a forward Connor. Get out there."*

Connor sprang to his feet as fast as I'd ever seen him, galloping onto the field, waving to everyone as if he was in the Rose Bowl Parade, yelping the whole way to the center of the field where the ref was standing. The ref blew the whistle and *Wham!* The ball was booted down the opposing team's field. All the boys took off running after it—all the boys except Connor. He stood there looking at the ref wondering if he was okay, since he had a frown on his face. Connor was concerned for him and immediately felt sad. In fact, he said, *"Are you okay?"* as parents and coaches were barking commands to their kids to go attack the ball.

Connor was oblivious to everything else going on. *"Get down there, Connor! Come on, Connor! Hustle, Connor! Go after the ball, Connor!"* the parents and coaches chanted. But Connor contently shadowed the ref as he moved around the field, focused on the ref's facial expression. Connor had no idea where the ball was, nor did he care. But it certainly seemed to irritate some of the parents. The coaches, who knew about his diagnosis of Williams, also seemed a bit irked, though they hid their frustration well. I mean, come on! It's about winning, right?

Some parents on the sidelines appeared confused. Others seemed visibly irritated that Connor hadn't blasted down the field with the other *normal* boys. I stood quietly behind them, some not knowing I was Connor's father. Then I heard one of the fathers say, "Look at that poor boy. He doesn't know *what's* going on. He doesn't get it. What's with that kid?"

At first blush, I wanted to go up to the guy, get in his face, and explain my son's situation so he felt like a raving idiot. But then I thought, surrender this one and let it go. So I did, at least I tried, though it made me sad for the rest of the day. I couldn't get the tape to stop playing, "Look at that poor boy. He doesn't know *what's* going on."

Things like this happen all the time. I was going to have to learn how to let them slide off my shoulders as best I knew how, though it did make me angry when parents would say these things. Even when they learned Connor was my son, they *still* had a hard time keeping their comments to themselves. As I said, some folks are harsh and very self-consumed. Winning is pretty important in our culture, just not to Connor. Feelings trump for him. These events are hard to shake off because they remind me of my son's challenges, though he's doing so well on many things. Yet the fact remains, he is challenged, and always will be.

I am learning when to speak up, and use it as a teaching point for those who aren't caregivers of special-needs children. I'm also learning when to keep my mouth shut, something harder than you can imagine, at least, if you're a defender of your children, which most parents are.

This is an example of the harshness that routinely comes off many of our tongues. Maybe this is where the expression comes from, *"Bite your tongue."* It's a good expression, and one I'm trying to follow, since I've come to believe that unless people have had a life-altering situation hit them, many of us are *clueless* about being sensitive to the emotional and mental health needs of caregivers. Instead, we cast hurt without even thinking, which takes caregivers time and energy to work through. As if they don't have *enough* on their plates to deal with already!

As the title of this chapter asks, *What am I to learn from this?* I guess, to be more gentle and focused on the other person first. It's easy to say, but hard to do, unless there's a consequence. *"Poor boy?"* No. Lucky father? Yes! I didn't used to feel that way but I do now. Was I being taught something, and maybe what to do with it?

Connor's imaginary friend, the "bug"

ACCEPT THE SITUATION AND FIND PEACE WITH IT

Find peace with it? That's hard for *anyone* when things don't go their way. Us grownups are often the worst when things don't roll the way we think they should. And things hadn't rolled right for me for years. Did I feel excused from needing to find some peace with my new life? Absolutely! But acceptance of my new charter as the single father of a beautiful and challenging special-needs child was coming to a peaceful place of rest inside—a new grace that friends noticed. Actually, they thought I'd become *way* too mellow, suggesting I revert back to the old me. Not possible. This was the new person, necessary to cope with and manage the swings in Connor's day, activities, and feelings. I had to stay loose, since I never knew when the next *thing* would hit. The *things* will, of course change, as he gets older. Never a dull moment with The Boylan Boys.

Social graces is a concept that doesn't always register with Connor, though he is high functioning. He doesn't comprehend what's appropriate when, nor does he necessarily care. Remember, his brain is not *wired* like yours. He doesn't have the same number of genes. So trying to teach him various things, so he understands what is appropriate when and why is hard. To Connor, it's all about love, feelings, spontaneity, and genuineness. Being authentic registers. There is no other way to Connor. How wonderfully disarming. Still, it causes people pretty set in their ways to get uncomfortable. There's probably something to learn here.

Summer was here, which in Minnesota can mean it won't snow for at least another week. Weather people are a hit in Minnesota since a normal conversation includes questions about what's in store weather-wise. This summery Saturday was gorgeous, and Connor and I were headed up to a friend's cabin for a day of relaxing, visiting, boating, and eating with cousins and good friends, an annual event we looked forward to. Connor was a great traveler, listening to any piece of music I put on as he studied the patterns of the song. He has amazing rhythm.

The drive went by quickly and he blasted out of the jeep yelling the names of his cousins, almost tackling them with his greeting. There were many fun people for Connor to chat and play with.

One particular man, I'll call him Bob, hadn't been there in years past so I don't think Connor had ever seen him before. A tremendous man, accomplished, professional, and formal, but that was his style. He was a kind and considerate man, always enjoyable to visit with. Remember, Connor doesn't understand personal boundaries very well at this stage in his life. After a fun day, Bob and his wife announced to everyone that they were going to head home. All of a sudden, Connor sprang to his feet, ran right at Bob, slamming into his legs, jolting him as he locked his arms around Bob's legs, saying at the top of his lungs, *"Bye Bob. Love you Bob."* Bob stood there surprised and stunned. Connor had invaded his space and touched him with his unfiltered love. You could see the surprise in Bob's eyes. It was a special moment; one I'm guessing Bob will never forget; how a challenged child broke through the formality and typical appropriate boundaries we all have to share some uncoached affection.

Would a *normal* child have done this? Maybe. Connor isn't affected by the *rules* of what's considered appropriate behavior, and in this case, it seemed a welcomed and tender surprise that ended up touching someone. It is amazing how he has this impact on people though he's mentally challenged. We can never have too much love, especially in this world.

"Bye Bob. Love you Bob." There will be many more situations like this in the years ahead, some pleasant and special like this one, others that will be tough to handle, based on what he does. And I will be there to witness the good intentions and hopefully—how they will be received.

Chapter Seventeen

WHERE'S THE HUMOR?

We all need humor. Sometimes, it's the only thing that can help us make it through. Yet for years, humor had hidden its face from me. I couldn't find any, in anything—a good comedy, a funny movie, or a clown at the circus. *Nothing* was funny anymore. Life was a series of serious events, usually draining and tough. Yet as I came to accept and find peace with my new life, the humor came from Connor. Sometimes not appropriate, but always genuine and harmless.

For example, one of my close friends and his wife referred their European cleaning lady and her company to me. They said she was a trustworthy person who had done a great job, so I thought I'd give her and her two helpers a try.

Never having met them, Connor ran to the front door of the house as a blond woman and two darker-haired ladies meekly approached. Once on the stoop, they looked through the glass, waiting patiently for him to let them in. Jumping up and down as if he'd never seen people before, Connor ripped open the front door, smiled and said, "Hello girls. Want to sleep over in my bed today?"

Not knowing about Conner, the blond glared at me, like I was some weirdo who couldn't be trusted. As if I'd put Connor up to saying such a thing!

I gently apologized, explaining that my son had special needs. They shrugged it off after they began to engage with him and realized that something about him was different, and oh so genuine.

Humor had to come back now for the sake of my own mental health, because life was even harder and more intense. Humor would have to be my new leveler, my chill-out gauge, and my barometer for finding a new pace with Connor. Humor was also something I used all the time to help him when he'd get stuck, a common occurrence.

Similar to someone with Alzheimer's, which I'm familiar with since I took care of my father's parents in their later years, Connor can be functioning at a high level and all of a sudden, he'll freeze. It's as if his brain goes dark, locks up, or goes on strike for a moment. I'll get the deer-in-the-headlights look, and know immediately what's going on. It's like he goes away momentarily, and sometimes, it's as if he doesn't know it's happening. Everything just stops—and then he'll come back. In these times, I remain gentle with humor at the ready, which sometimes helps pull him back from wherever he went for a while.

Where's the humor in my story? There isn't any really, but it's being offered up to you and others who may or may not be a caregiver, with the hope that by sharing it, others will find solace and hope as they manage through the sometimes intensely difficult times caregivers can face throughout their lifetime. And to acknowledge that, without humor or being able to *find* humor in our darkest hours; then we *are* in trouble. It's that important to our mental health and overall desire to move forward.

Connor often does very funny things as he goes about his day, and what makes them so special is that he's not trying to be funny, but real. And *that* is the coolest part for me. The unbridled rawness of real!

CHAPTER EIGHTEEN

LAYING NEW CEMENT—MANAGING THE SETBACKS WITH GRACE

At 49 years old, I'm starting over in one sense. But in another, I have a story meant to uplift others experiencing similar struggles over mind, heart, and their desire to move forward as they care for their special-needs children, or deal with another intense time calling for massive strength.

Whereas I thought I had a solid foundation under me, it seems that for some reason (which I believe will be revealed in the years ahead), it's been busted up with a jackhammer, as I lay down fresh cement underneath my new life. A foundation that will be more secure and enduring as it hardens up underneath a more empathetic heart, which has been changed. And the setbacks? There have been many; so many and so frequent, that it felt as though I was being used for target practice on a never-ending hunt, until I turned myself over to someone who I believe has been hunting me for a long time. Perhaps to do more important work for the benefit of many in need.

I'll manage the setbacks ahead—and there will be plenty—as Connor grows and experiences life. And I am focused on assisting caregivers (who may be wondering if they'll ever get any relief) of special-needs children in the trenches day in and day out. I've been there—am there—and know what it feels like. Helping them make it through seems a worthwhile endeavor. At the end of the day, isn't *this* what it's all about — helping others get over the humps in life to a better place?

If you're not a caregiver, how will you help? Surely you can do something. So what would that be? And if you are a caregiver, get into **The RFM Network™** so you begin getting the support and encouragement you need, from other like-minded caregivers of special-needs children. We can all help each other, which *is* the grand design.

When everything hit for me, I couldn't see anything forward. There were no pictures ahead, as I mentioned. Just fog so thick you could have cut it with a knife. There was no clear direction for which way my boat should sail, as there was no wind. But with grace and guidance, I was slowly brought through the fire. I've got some nice burns, but nothing I haven't learned to handle if I'm centered and calm.

Can I tell you that all the flames have been put out? No they haven't. There are still some that are smoldering as I look for new pictures and new experiences with Connor that I believe will create the path ahead. Is this approach too fuzzy? Not at all, as I am done attempting to forge ahead with my own plan, without the guidance and grace from above, helping show me and reinforce the right way to go.

I've hit *way* too many cement walls over the past several years to forge ahead without asking for guidance. If that's too gooey for you, I understand. But for me, it's how I've come to learn that someone else is ultimately in charge, and that I need to do a better job of listening to that voice and following through with what I hear. Again, not exactly the Type A, kick-butt and take-some-names personality that I learned was important in the business world, but rather, a wiser approach. Involving Him in my planning by asking for guidance. Something I can honestly say I wasn't doing a whole bunch of for the first 25 years.

Again, if that is too gushy for you, that's okay. I'm sharing what I've learned. However, what I believe at this point, after all the hardship and knowing there are more tough times ahead, is that if we just have the faith to ask—and then listen—we will be shown how to make it through. It's like a steady light guiding you along day by day, as you're ready to walk just a little bit farther, to a place where you *know* you'll be alright—that you *can* do it! And that you *will* do it! You *will* move forward creating new and better pictures ahead. Not because you have no choice in the matter, because you do! But perhaps you've never considered this perspective, as I never did when I was thrashing around for answers.

Perhaps YOU have been called. Called for an *extra* level of service to and for your special-needs children, or someone very dear to you. And through your service and care, you'll be given an understanding of life and love that is so deep and so real, that you will feel the hand of the Almighty on your shoulder as he looks you in the face and says, *"You can do this. You will do this. I will give you the strength you need and it will come from the love and care you give to your Angel Child."*

There are pictures ahead for you. Believe that. I have, and continue to feel the warmth of that belief, because it does help you move forward. So trust that perhaps *you* have been given a special dispensation—an Angel Child—and that you are already closer than most to seeing what the face and hands of the Creator feel like, as you open up to and embrace the new pictures in store for you. Be blessed—and hold your Angel Child.

Gretchen, one of Connor's ski instructors at Challenge Aspen

Christmas morning—Santa ate the cookie we left out for him!

Graduation from second grade

First day at Music and Dance camp—Challenge Aspen

The Cowboy Hoedown at the T-Lazy 7 Ranch

Beverly, one of Connor's ski instructors at Challenge Aspen

THE CONNOR PRINCIPLES™—GUIDEPOSTS FOR EVERYDAY LIFE

In a tragedy or traumatic event, there are lessons that can be taken away from the situation and hopefully applied in the times ahead. Sometimes these lessons don't come all at once, but rather, are revealed over time; maybe as we're ready to receive, understand, and *do something* with them, so we don't make the same mistakes again. Or perhaps it's so that we adjust ourselves for the times ahead, becoming stronger, wiser, and deeper, with a more complete perspective from the experience.

That said, I was sitting in a lawn chair crying and reflecting on all that had happened—yellow notepad in my lap, pen in hand. I was staring out over the ocean during a gorgeous sunset, asking for guidance and relief, when these principles came gushing into my head. I didn't have to figure them out, organize them into a manner that made sense, or even name them. They came that way—in a specific order, each with their own key point and three-word slogan, making them easy to remember. The ten came in one conscious stream—that fast. I needed to get out of the way and not micromanage the information, since it was coming from the best communicator of information the world has ever known. Better not mess with that.

I let the information flow onto the paper in the manner it seemed designed, to teach, comfort, and bring hope, so that when applied, they could actually manifest these things. And I believe they will, with trust and belief in the person who brought them to and through me—to you! Intense? Not really. Powerful? Yes. Simple? That's their beauty.

As you read *The Connor Principles™*, remember who they're ultimately coming from, and let them be of comfort to you in your current situation and the future. Remember the passages from Rick Warren's book *The Purpose Driven Life*:

> "God uses problems to draw you closer to himself. The Bible says, The Lord is close to the brokenhearted; he rescues those who are crushed in spirit. Your most profound and intimate experiences of worship will likely be in your darkest days—when your heart is broken, when you feel abandoned, when you're out of options, when the pain is great—and you turn to God alone. It is during suffering that we learn to pray our most authentic, heartfelt, honest-to-God prayers. Problems force us to look to God

and depend on him instead of ourselves. You'll never know that God is all you need until God is all you've got!

There's a Grand Designer behind everything. Your life is not a result of random chance, fate, or luck. There is a master plan. God is pulling the strings. God's plan for your life involves all that happens to you— including your mistakes, your sins, and your hurts. Under pressure, your faith-life is forced into the open and shows its true colors."

THE CONNOR PRINCIPLES™

GUIDEPOSTS FOR EVERYDAY LIFE

RELEASE THE ANGER

I don't care who you are. When the news hits that you have a child with special needs—perhaps *profound* special needs, and that it may *forever* alter your life moving forward, you *are* going to get mad! Downright angry in fact! No matter how reserved or introverted your personality and temperament, you *will* get angry. If you disagree or feel I'm over-blowing the situation, it's perhaps because you're not being that honest with yourself yet.

It's okay to get angry and frustrated. For crying out loud, what's wrong with that, when you receive news that your child might or does have a special-needs diagnosis? It's news that will beyond a shadow of a doubt, alter, change, or prevent some or most of the dreams, expectations, and goals you've had for your life from *ever* being realized. That's a pretty good reason to get angry. It's more than a slight curve ball you've been thrown. It's a curve ball that never stops curving! More like a knuckle ball since, with a special-needs child, you don't know what's coming next.

Now that we've established that you're going to get angry numerous times over the years to come, and that it's okay to feel that way about the situations life has handed you, learning how to deal with and release it is not only important, but essential to your own mental health going forward—and that of your family's.

That said—do I have some formula, or time-tested process that will help release the anger? Absolutely not. It is something I struggle with as well. Everyone has to find their own way in which they can essentially release the anger and frustrations that come with life-altering news about a special-needs child;

the shock and numbness you feel, the sense of hopelessness, despair, and utter sadness. And all of the new realities that have to be faced over time, that you may never again have the life you've had up until the time of the diagnosis. It's a whole new ball game now, with new players.

Is it selfish to be angry when you get the news? Who cares? You may have received incredibly difficult news that may take years to digest. Yes, years. I am *still* digesting the news about Connor's diagnosis, and it's been seven years. I still find myself in scenarios where I'm bothered about something I can't do because of my life as a caregiver of a special-needs child. Is that selfish? Sure, but I don't beat myself up about it, nor should you. Cut yourself some slack once in a while. It is hard!

What I'm learning is that I'll probably have these feelings from time to time for the rest of my life, that it's okay, and that I need to learn how to cope with and manage them in order to stay focused on my son. I need to remain optimistic to the future as he grows and remember that I've been *called* (maybe you've been called too) for an extra level of service, which you can't deliver if you're angry all the time. This belief has helped me cope. Maybe it will help you too.

Anger can be dangerous to you, your friends, family, coworkers, and your special-needs children. So, for their own sakes and yours, find some help if you or others close to you feel you need it, so you can release it. Sometimes, the only people able to comprehend how hard and lonely it is being a caregiver are other caregivers. They get it—the pain, frustration, the sense of loss. They also struggle, as I do, with not wanting to come across as a complainer. Yet they'd also like to have a *life* once in a while, since it's normal to feel as though theirs was radically altered. Fellow caregivers *get* the anger thing and the importance of needing to release it.

Releasing the anger can bring a new level of peace and acceptance about all the unknowns that lie ahead, so you can handle them in stride, growing deeper, more resilient, and stronger. Find a way to release it, over, and over, and over again. Make it part of your daily regime of moving forward, so that you can.

As I mentioned, doubt, or worse yet, self-doubt, which can come upon you out of nowhere when you receive life-altering news, is not only a paralyzing drug, but one that can stop your life in its tracks on all levels. And *that* hurts your special-needs children, and your family.

NOBODY—no self-help guru, motivational speaker, prince, princess, president, queen, king, ambassador, professional actor, athlete, or the like, has any better *fix* or approach on handling doubt or self-doubt than you or me. In fact, here's a unique way to consider things: perhaps as caregivers of special-needs children, we have had *more* than our fair share of surprises and life interruptions. And because of this, we've been *forced* to deal with more intense levels of self-doubt than others. So maybe *we* are better prepared than most to cope with it when it arises. It's something worth looking at, since many of us have had to wrestle with so much of it on an ongoing basis, throughout the course of our lives as caregivers.

Doubt, like anger, can essentially ruin your life because it can strip away the joy sitting right in front of you for you to experience through your special-needs child. But if you're all hosed up inside, you're locked out from experiencing anything. You *must* find a way to release the doubts that may have filled your head and heart, to someone who has more power than us all.

Do I have doubts? Absolutely. They are part of our everyday existence. So learning to somehow block them as best we can from overtaking your person, is critically important in helping you accept and embrace the new life that lies ahead, with all its twists and turns.

ACCEPT THE LOVE

How nice would it be if we could learn to accept another person's love when it doesn't come in the form or fashion we think it should—a gesture of appreciation or affection toward us without trying to control, filter, or micromanage how it is shown? That would be a huge lesson, though merely just a fantasy perhaps, being how *concerned* most of us are about how things *look* and the *appearance* of this or that needing to be just so—at least in *our* opinion. And you thought most of us weren't interested in control. Think that one through again!

This is another lesson from Connor's world. He is cognitively challenged with his diagnosis of Williams, though high functioning in many areas at the present time. But he understands one thing very well—the giving of love unconditionally. He doesn't understand the concept of a stranger. There is no such thing in his world. Everyone is a friend who should be loved. I have watched him approach people he's never seen before with the warmest of greetings, only to watch many of these people (mostly adults) not accept his warmth, but rather, angle on what's wrong with him. Accept his love? No. They're trying to figure out what's the matter with him. And the love? It goes right by them. It was intended for them, no question there. But they couldn't accept it. Why? I wish I knew. Are *you* like that? Can you accept the love? If not, go hang out with some special-needs children in your area tomorrow, and they'll quickly teach you what it's all about, though they're just being themselves. Interesting what we can all learn from children born with *less* than what we have, in one sense.

Good or bad, many special-needs children don't know how to worry. It doesn't register. They know love. It's what they understand and give. And maybe, just maybe, we could be happier and more comforted if we learned, as they already know, how to accept the love. It is there for you to experience, even in the times you might be going through right now. Accept it, and find a new level of peace.

GIVE TO GIVE

As I've mentioned, Connor has approached people he's never seen before with open arms and a total trust in them, wanting to greet them, hug them, give them something—only to be rejected in more than a few cases. Rebuffed and shunned. It is *so* hard to watch. He'll look at me with total confusion. But he doesn't really comprehend (at his current stage of development) the notion of being rejected, so he'll often come right back at the person who has rejected his gestures with the same heartfelt intent of wanting to give them his greeting and whatever else he was intending to give.

Giving to give for the simple genuine tenderness of giving. It's taken people aback, and melted away their defensiveness. What power. Giving to give.

Connor doesn't understand lashing back at people if they don't receive him kindly, something I dare say many of us are pretty good at, if we're being honest. Maybe this is because when he's giving, he isn't looking for whatever he's going to get in return. There's no expectation there. By watching him give to give, I have seen him melt away the snarls, hurt, and anger in people's faces, replacing them with a warm blanket of lotion spread across the person's soul. It's really kind of transformational when you see it.

Giving to give. Something I was taught as a young boy as the right way to approach people. I don't know where it changed along the way, the notion of holding back until you know exactly whom you're dealing with. But it's a lesson that's been made real for me by my son, a boy with less cognitive ability than many, and perhaps more emotional and heartfelt capacity than most.

How much can we learn *and* gain from others when we focus first on giving to give, versus giving to get? Basic stuff I know, and yet it took my mentally challenged son to drive it home for me. What about you? Something we can all practice more of—giving to give.

APPROACH THE CLOSED

Who am I talking about? People like me! Allow me to explain. When we got the news about Connor, I gradually shut down and closed myself off from the world over a number of years. The emotional trauma and mental exhaustion, which I had no experience in coping with, was hard for me to handle. I became closed off without even being aware of it. As a result, my family, friends, coworkers, and clients didn't know how to approach me anymore. What to say? How to act? They were as confused about how to approach me, and my new situation, as I was hurting and closed off.

Though I've mentioned it already, I find it stunning that research says I am one of approximately 35 million people in the United States who are parents or related caregiver to a special-needs child. Imagine how many caregivers might be in the process of shutting down or closing themselves off emotionally, psychologically, or spiritually?

When caregivers shut down, it impacts **everyone**—the family, the special-needs children, and all employer organizations. That's the scope of how it touches society, business, industry, and governments—local, state, and federal. The **financial ramifications** to all of us are something to take notice of. And how it will touch us in the future, if caregivers don't get the emotional support, respite, and ongoing encouragement they need?

Shutting down and closing off from the world was my situation for years, and I'm certainly not unique in this area. On any given day, there are probably millions of caregivers of special-needs children who, at any one time, are in serious need of support from someone who has the emotional bandwidth to walk with them during challenging and lonely times.

Caregiver or not, we can learn to help each other (since the scope of this issue is enormous and ever-growing), by understanding the massive stress and "bat-to-the-head" feeling that news of a child diagnosed with a special need transfers to the parents. By *attempting* to comprehend this level of shock, sadness, and hopelessness, perhaps you will reach out and approach a caregiver before they close themselves off from the world, helping them, their family, and their special-needs children. It's as critical as any humanitarian relief effort, right here in our own country. Look around! This issue is all around us.

Approach the closed. Oftentimes, those you approach won't understand they've closed themselves off from the world around them. They might want to be held, walked with, encouraged, or listened to. And you can do this if you're someone who understands compassion. They're either coping with devastating news, and/or getting used to carrying a new cross. If you step in and help them carry it once in a while, you will help them find a new resilience within themselves to carry on and move forward as best they can.

Approach the closed. It *always* comes back to help you because it's the right thing to do!

OPEN YOUR MIND

Connor and I were all dressed up in downtown Minneapolis during the Christmas season, enjoying a holiday concert at Orchestra Hall featuring the fabulous and talented Doc Severinsen conducting the orchestra. It's one of the traditions our family enjoys during the holidays.

I am always on edge during these beautiful concerts because, although Connor *lives* for music of all kinds, the sound of any saxophone or high-pitched trumpet can send him over the edge due to his massive sensitivity to certain loud and high-pitched sounds. As a safety precaution, I brought along his sound-deadening headphones, to prevent him from going into orbit if he heard any of these sounds, though it's hard to predict when they were coming.

Connor was having a wonderful time, proud to be a part of all the music, while watching his grandma Judy (my mom) sing in the choir. The first half went without interruption, but toward the end of the second half, Doc let his horn rip, hitting a high note for a prolonged period. I knew the song so I was prepared, clamping on his headphones in plenty of time. But it didn't do the trick this time. Connor heard the note, grabbed his ears over his headphones and starting kicking the seats in front of us, tears streaming down his cheeks. I picked him up, all 85 pounds, and quickly brought him out into the adjoining hallway, away from the loud trumpet sounds. I held him as he rocked back and forth, hands opening and closing in rapid succession, repeating how his ears hurt—and that he wanted to go back in and watch more. It is *unbelievably* challenging sometimes when these things occur, which is on a routine basis.

As people were leaving after the concert, we got the chance to go back stage and mingle with the orchestra, choir, and Doc Severinsen. Standing in line as patiently as Connor knew how, holding my hand and attempting to wait, something *very* difficult for him to do, as he asked repeatedly what we were waiting for, he took off. He broke through a crowd of people and security standing between Doc, and us, who I could see leaning in the doorway of a dressing room visiting with well-wishers. I took off after Connor, catching up with him just as he ran up to Doc, bear-hugging him, interrupting his conversation with other well-wishers, and said, *"You play too loud. Hurts my ears."* Can you imagine Johnny Carson saying that to Doc? Doc, being the gracious person he is, could see Connor rocking back and forth, and more than likely picked up that he might be a special-needs child. He engaged Connor in conversation, apologizing for playing his trumpet too loud as others looked on with astonishment that I would allow my child to speak to an accomplished musician in such a disrespectful manner! The looks I got were harsh. But Doc handled it all in perfect stride, not only by being kind and gentle, but also by engaging with him.

Appropriate exchange? For a special-needs child it can be typical, because you never know what they're going to say or do from time to time. What it did for me is teach me how "on edge" many of us are, including me, about what's appropriate, what's not, and that as a people, we've got little tolerance for *any* variation on what we view as acceptable behavior. We can be harshly closed-minded about anything out of the ordinary, which this story was. Still, Doc seemed to find it delightfully refreshing—the honesty of it all.

This story, one of hundreds I could share, reminds me of how closed-minded I can be at times, which prevents me from the fuller experience I believe Connor is teaching me about life. I'm learning that it's okay, maybe even healthy, to open my mind to new experiences that perhaps aren't going to happen necessarily in the *appropriate* manner. It is okay to loosen up a bit, open my mind, and enjoy the ride that Connor is taking me on.

If you allowed yourself to open your mind a bit more, what new experiences could you enjoy that might enrich your life and learning?

TRUST THE GUIDANCE

As a caregiver of a special-needs child, you're going to get lots of advice, suggestions, opinions, and guidance from lots of people: doctors, lawyers, researchers, clinicians, licensed therapists, teachers, paraprofessionals, counselors, mental health professionals, specialists, your parents, brothers, sisters, extended family members, your priest, minister, rabbi, therapist, and on and on and on. Some guidance will be welcomed and some not, as everyone has an opinion on how to parent a special-needs child—even those who don't have one!

Be that as it may, only *you* will know for sure as you digest all the advice; what guidance is right for you, your special-needs children and your family. So trust yourself, which is sometimes hard to do when you've been shaken up and down like a salt and peppershaker. Trust your instincts on the guidance that feels right to you.

You are going to go through periods where it may seem as though your whole life is being challenged; your outlook, your nature, the manner in which you've been managing your life, etc. In my case, it caused me to surrender, as I've shared earlier, to the notion that perhaps I was not the ultimate person in control, inviting more guidance than ever before. And I have trusted that guidance as a road map for the new life I am now trying to carve out of the experiences and life situations that have entered my life's path, with the hope that by offering them up, they will benefit many others on their path.

CARVE YOUR FUTURE

Before Connor's birth and the news of his diagnosis, the future as I saw it was pretty clear. Everything seemed to be in its rightful place and on track, as we love to say—the lingo for letting others and ourselves know we're in a good place. But when the diagnosis came, all of those plans and pictures went away overnight, and I lived for a period of *years* with no clear picture of what the future held for me, my family, or my special-needs child. I was essentially in a trance.

This can be a dangerous reality for any man, especially those who are hard charging, task-oriented, get-it-done type people. I cannot speak to how women process information when there are constant ups and downs and everything seems up in the air and totally fuzzy. I think it's safe to say, however, that *nobody* enjoys extended periods of confusion, anxiety, and uncertainty about their future. But for caregivers of special-needs children, they must live from day to day with higher levels of uncertainty about the future. Sometimes this causes anxiety, depression, or anger. Other times it can cause people to surrender a bit—opening up to receiving help from others, or from above, in those cases when you feel you have no one else to turn to for strength.

That being said, at some point, you will need to start carving your new future; new pictures, new dreams, new plans, a new or different work life that can better accommodate your responsibilities as a caregiver. You'll also need new family traditions around your life with a special-needs child. It won't all come together at once; so don't expect that it will. But after you process the initial trauma, the learning process begins. All the emotional adjustments begin to settle in your heart, and you start to regain some level of normalcy—if you dare call it that. And when this time comes, you'll intuitively know it's time for you to begin carving your new future; that you can do it, and you will do it, because you have *way* too much to share that will help many others.

SHARE YOUR EXPERIENCE

As children, we're taught to share. That it's not only important, but what life is really all about. But sadly, as we grow into adulthood, this early teaching seems to get pushed to the wayside of life.

As caregivers of special-needs children, I believe we've been given the calling of sharing our challenges, stories, doubts, fears, and special moments with other caregivers that could benefit from learning about our lives—and what we've learned as a result. I'm not suggesting you become a motivational speaker. But more than likely, there are things you've learned along your path that could help others on theirs.

Some people believe that intense hardships, challenges, or extreme difficulties actually sculpt the heart, soul, and character of a person into a more complete picture of who they're designed to be. If you are one who believes in this line of thinking, then trust that your experience is worth sharing. Your lessons could be of genuine benefit to others. Consider sharing your experience. Isn't *that* what life is all about?

EMBRACE YOUR CHILD

Everybody gets surprises thrown at them during their lifetime. Some are small and relatively easy to deal with. Others are more significant, often causing pain, anxiety, stress, maybe even a setback or two. But over a relatively short period of time, you learn to deal with the surprise or disappointment, and move through the experience, hopefully to a better place.

When you're the parent of a special-needs child, however, it's a PERMANENT surprise! One that raises the bar on all sorts of emotions, some you never knew you had. It can totally eclipse you. I've seen it happen with caregivers, including me. It can be such a *permanent life jolt* that some can't recover—can't get back on the horse of life. This can become a serious issue for the caregiver, their family, and the special-needs children if not resolved or dealt with in some manner.

In these situations, a huge level of resentment can come out toward the special-needs child, family or spouse—none of which deserve it because it's not anyone's fault. Instead of fostering resentment toward your special-needs child because your world may now be turned upside down, I have learned to slow way down, cut back on, or cut out, any activities that add to the stress of life with your special-needs child. This helps you embrace them, and learn from them.

If that sounds too rosy, perhaps getting some professional help might be a solution. It can help you learn to calm down, get rid of the toxic resentments toward life or whomever, and prepare you to experience the true power of what special-needs children can teach us all.

Don't push them away because you're resentful that your life might now be stressful, complex, and hard. It's not always going to be that way, and **it's not their fault!** Get help with these legitimate feelings so you can experience and embrace your special-needs child.

Forward Communications is a unique community of people addressing one of the most compelling issues of our time facing millions of people—and all employer organizations.

Based on credible research, as many as **one** in **five** families in the U.S. (20 percent) is a parent or a related caregiver to a special-needs child. This translates to upwards of 35 million people impacted daily in numerous ways. It also directly impacts (financially) employer organizations in the areas of medical claims, insurance premiums, morale, absenteeism and turnover, creativity, sense of spirit and ability to focus, and level of enthusiasm on the job.

Between 5 and 10 percent of an organization's total employee population can be caregivers of special-needs children, shedding light on why the issue directly impacts the financial health and productivity of all corporations.

Forward Communications is addressing this broad-reaching issue through something called **The Reach For Me (rfm) Network™**, which is essentially two things. Firstly, it's an online interactive community of caregivers of special-needs children sharing their challenges, knowledge, stories, inspiration, emotional support, and encouragement with other like-minded caregivers, providing a web of support, trust, and ongoing encouragement for millions of caregivers.

Over time, it will also become a physical network in local communities throughout the country, where caregivers can attend weekly support group meetings with other parents of special-needs children. Trusted Advisors, who are professionally licensed, certified, and trained to facilitate meetings focused on taking care of the caregiver, will host these weekly meetings.

Mission And Purpose

To provide a network of ongoing emotional and psychological support, encouragement, information, inspiration, and friendship for like-minded people who share a common bond—parents and related caregivers of special-needs children—sharing hope, understanding, and knowledge through the online interactive community and weekly outreach meetings, and through their employer organizations via corporate enterprise memberships in The rfm Network™ for their own employee caregivers.

The purpose is to reduce employee-caregiver absenteeism and turnover, burnout, medical claims of all kinds, insurance premiums and related costs to employer organizations, while increasing productivity, focus, attitude, loyalty, and commitment to the enterprise. In essence, **taking care of the caregiver**, so they can take better care of their special-needs children and be more productive for the organizations that employ them.

Forward Communications is dedicated to helping caregivers and employer organizations deal with sudden, unexpected, significant life events that happen from time to time. This includes helping caregivers find emotional support, encouragement, and inspiration so they can move forward with a renewed sense of passion and commitment, becoming more resourceful to themselves, their families, and the organizations who employ them. It's a win-win approach for employee-caregivers, organizations, and communities.

Fortune 2000 and mid-sized organizations can purchase a **Corporate Enterprise Membership** in The RFM Network™, allowing employee-caregivers within that organization to join the network at no charge. This allows employee-caregivers the option to participate as they desire in the online interactive community. This provides employee-caregivers (5+ percent of total employee population) the support they need on an ongoing basis.

The financial benefit to the organization is clear: enhanced employee loyalty, productivity, and commitment to the enterprise, as well as a reduction in absenteeism, turnover, insurance claims, premiums, and litigation, which all cost organizations dearly.

For a complete listing of products, services, programs, and corporate membership options for organizations of all sizes, please visit our Web site, **www.Forward–Communications.com**

JOIN THE GROUNDSWELL

If you are a **senior executive** with an employer organization, contact us to discuss **corporate membership options** in The RFM Network™. Your membership will allow employee-caregivers within your own company to join the network at no charge. They'll receive the emotional support, encouragement, recognition, and inspiration they need to keep moving forward.

If you are a **caregiver**, join The RFM Network™ and start receiving the emotional support and ongoing encouragement you deserve to help you keep moving forward in very challenging times.

If you are a **licensed marriage** or **family therapist**, psychologist, mental health professional or the like, learn how to become a **Trusted Advisor** in the network. The relationships and referrals you build could increase your annual client billings by 5 to 10 percent or more, helping grow your professional practice. To learn more, visit the Web site and click on **Become a Trusted Advisor**.

Book The Author For Your Organization's Next Event or Meeting

The founder of Forward Communications, Michael A. Boylan, is one of the most engaging and qualified keynote speakers in the country, having addressed groups from a few hundred to 7,000 attendees. He consistently receives high marks from all organizations because of his interactive style and the lasting value participants feel they have received.

Michael can tailor his address to meet the objectives of your meeting. To learn more regarding keynote rates and availability, contact Forward Communications LLC at the number below.

Contact Us

Forward Communications LLC
Carlson Center, 601 Carlson Parkway, Suite 1050
Minnetonka, Minnesota, 55305
Office: 952–449–5115 Fax: 952–856–4898
Web Site: www.Forward–Communications.com

You may have noticed the picture on the back cover of the book—Connor and I walking toward the location of this amazing summer music and dance camp for special-needs children, which I have taken Connor to for the last four summers. This camp, in addition to the ski program in which I have enrolled him, is helping his overall cognitive, fine, and gross motor growth. He loves the program and always looks forward to going. I speak as a father of a special-needs child, and as a "customer" of the program. I know the founder and management. They are committed people, focused around giving your child a wonderful, memory-rich, safe, and fun experience.

It's called "Challenge Aspen," a year-round, nonprofit offering recreational, cultural, competitive, and educational opportunities for children with cognitive or physical disabilities. Check out the Web site at www.ChallengeAspen.com. The office phone is 970-923-0578.